VICTORY

Words by John WILLIAMS

Images by Tom STODDART

BOOKMAN
PUBLISHERS

VICTORY

With TONY BLAIR on the Road to a Landslide

First published 1997 by

Bookman Publishers

Floor 22

1 Canada Square

Canary Wharf

London E14 5AP

Design, editing and production by International Publishing Associates

Art Director: Anne Rowe

Scanning and Image Quality: John Symonds

The publishers would like to thank Richard Holledge and David Waldman for their assistance

in the production of this book

ISBN 1 898718 84 9

1 2 3 4 5 6 7 8 9

Contents

Foreword

THE 1997 general election was not so much a landslide as an earthquake. As with real earthquakes, nobody suspected they were sitting on it until the earth suddenly moved. Most of us had missed the evidence all around us that Labour was going to bury the Conservatives.

Tony Blair told me the day before polling that he expected to win by a majority of 30. I believe he meant it. Though he may have been talking down his own expectations, he adamantly refused to believe in a landslide.

Like the rest of us, he was first shocked and then awed by the shifting of the political landscape in the early hours of May 2.

I spent the whole campaign following Tony Blair across the country and picked up no sense along the way of the scale of the victory he was winning. Now it is all over, there is a temptation to go back and inject some hindsight wisdom. I have resisted the temptation, because this was always meant to be an account that carried the real flavour of the election, as it was at the time.

Bear this in mind when puzzled by my unperceptively cautious mood along the way. This is how it felt. One day, when we have grown used to thinking of 1997 as earlier generations thought of 1945, it will be hard to recall how little we expected Blair's Earthquake. I am convinced that he certainly didn't. Like all veterans of the 1992 Labour defeat, he was determined not to be deluded again.

He set out expecting to win, but knowing it might yet go wrong. He was sure of victory in the second half of the campaign, but could not bring himself to believe that the huge poll leads were right.

Once Labour has been in power for a while, it will be hard to remember how it felt in those years when defeat had entered the Labour Party's soul and anything but Conservative government was unimaginable. Once Tony Blair has been Prime Minister for a time, he will seem to have always been inevitable, as history does once written down. There was nothing inevitable about those 15 hours between the close of polling and the new Prime Minister's arrival at Number Ten.

This is not meant to be a comprehensive account of the election. There were many elections taking place at once - at Labour's Millbank HQ, at Conservative Central Office, among the doorstep activists, on John Major's bus and Tony Blair's. There was only one place I wanted to be. This is an account of the winner's journey to Number Ten.

When we set out, I told Tony Blair he had better win - an account written from the loser's bus would be a bit odd. He said he would do his best. I reminded him from time to time on the road. On election night, as he made his jubilant way out of Trimdon Labour Club, he saw me in the crowd, put a hand on my shoulder and said: "The book's going to be all right then."

John Williams, Weston, Hertfordshire,
3 May, 1997.

THE CANDIDATE

FROM inside the Candidate's battle-bus, the cheers of the waiting crowd sound muffled and distant. The separateness of the Candidate's private world is exaggerated by his tinted windows. The real world looks distant and strange. The Candidate works in a small compartment at the back of the bus that feels like a cross between office and sitting room. It is more cramped than the head of any successful organisation would normally tolerate. Two sofas face each other across a table strewn with newspapers and notes, the debris that builds up through long hours ceaselessly on duty.

There is a fax machine in one corner, keeping Tony Blair in touch with campaign headquarters, and a television in the other, keeping him in touch with the world of the voter. The Candidate must never forget that the campaign that really matters is not his frenetic world of handshakes and speeches, interviews and hospital visits, instant decisions in response to calls from HQ. The real campaign is what comes down the tube into people's living rooms. He has to keep in touch with the greater reality of the TV campaign if he is to know how he is doing. Which 20 seconds of his endless day make the bulletins and what impact will they have? He has to create a believable version of himself for the public, but his success in doing so is determined by the bulletin editors who choose the words and pictures that the millions see.

On the wall of Tony Blair's mobile living room hangs a change of shirt - white, of course. Always, in public, the Candidate wears the crisp white shirt of leadership. One of the many uncredited heroes and heroines of Tony Blair's campaign is his mother-in-law, Gale, who keeps the Candidate supplied with freshly laundered shirts.

When the bus pulls into town, the Candidate and his wife make their way to the front of the vehicle. He pulls on his jacket and clips on his

> He is so intense that when his wife and staff chatter he doesn't hear them. He has the look on his face that he has on stage. The leadership look.

personal mike. While he is down among the crowd, the mike will relay his smalltalk to the reporters wearing headphones. Through the tinted windows, Tony Blair can see the faces of the people and hear their muffled cheering. He can see the same shop fronts, wherever he goes - McDonald's, Kwiksave, Marks and Spencer, Next. He sees the same faces on the photographers' stand. The door opens and the quality of sound changes to the din of a live audience, which is an unpredictable beast.

His staff alight first. Then he makes his way down the bus's steps and a bigger cheer goes up as the crowd sights him. He raises a hand and jumps down. It must feel like the moment when a swimmer plunges into cold water, knowing he dare not hesitate. Looking fitter and younger than most of the shopping centre crowd, he bounds up on to the box that serves as a travelling platform and says :"Hello, Luton..." or "Hello, Brentford...." or "Hello, Monmouth...."

There is no escaping the tyranny of the campaign speech. It has to be given, again and again. Nobody has a new script for every town; it can't be done and anyway, that's not the point of the town-square address. Once the campaign has settled down, so this regulation speech does too. It is better for being familiar, though up on their stand the photographers mimmick and laugh at the lines they know well, the lines the crowds cheer because they haven't heard them before: "We're going to give new hope to those young people, who should have decent jobs."

Tony Blair manages to say it with conviction each time. Unlike the photographers, he needs the crowd to believe in him and he knows he will have to deliver if they elect him. He knows that behind the instinctive suspicion of all politicians, the crowds long for something to believe in and he is it. This is the burden he carries alone. The policies he lists at each stop - smaller classes, youngsters off the dole, re-build the NHS - are the ones he painstakingly chose months ago in the knowledge that they would have to enthuse

the crowds he would meet. That too is a burden he has carried alone.

"Those young people," he says, pointing to the youngsters chanting Toe-Knee, Toe-Knee, Toe-Knee.

"They're this country's future". Usually one of the travelling press will mutter: "God Help this country".

The press that follows him likes this version of the Candidate least. They prefer the quiet, intelligent lectures, or the commanding, unscripted performances he has evolved and perfected during the campaign. They have a propri-etorial feel about the unscripted Tony Blair and, when he does an off-the-cuff press conference to impress the London commentators, the travel-ling press have a superior air, almost as if they helped the Candidate work out this acclaimed style.

But Blair himself insists he enjoys these town-square performances, which last only four or five minutes at most. Although the crowds are full of ordinary people - who regard him as "that man on the telly", like a soap star - the party is efficient at gathering members to cheer him on.

The atmosphere is good. He encoun-ters no hostility, though, as polling day nears, the Tories get better at sending hecklers. The Candidate loves them. He uses them.

"I'll tell you the problem, my friends - the country has rumbled you, they have found you out, they don't want any more of you."

Or, when youngsters are sent to chant against him: "They look all of 22 - that's one year for every Tory tax rise."

The photographers like that because they haven't heard it before. When he says something new they say: "New line alert! New line alert!"

Tony Blair finishes his speech, gets down from his box and shakes hands. Cherie follows him. The media would kill for a word from her. To the crowds, she is a mystery because she has never spoken to a newspaper or TV interviewer, but she speaks to them as she shakes hands. The crowds like her. She seems nice for someone so successful in her own right.

While the Candidate is among the people, the battlebus is a quiet place. The engine is off and the lights out.

Above: Tony Blair in a quiet moment before a speech. A cup of tea was never very far away.

Now the Candidate returns and the lights and air conditioning come on, with the engine. The bus begins to back away from the people, whose cheers are muffled again as the door closes. Tony Blair comes to the back of the bus. There is no trace of excitement or strain - he has switched off the public speaker, reverting to the alert campaign chief who needs to know what's going on. All the time he was on the stump, his staff have been on the phone. If it is true that mobile phones damage your health, Alastair Campbell, his press secretary, is a dead man.

The election never stops moving. In mid-afternoon, tomorrow is already being planned: the theme to grab the initiative and keep it all day, with luck. Never for a moment can anyone relax; nobody can ever tell which small problem may suddenly become the campaign nightmare, or which small opening the great opportunity to kill off your opponent.

The Candidate never has long to concentrate on any one thing. He has to have the kind of brain that can switch moment to moment from grand strategy to trivia. He would be rich if he charged for every time he is asked how many Spice Girls he can name - he can do them all now. He needs to pack every spare minute with interviews and tactical planning. He never gets enough time to think, never enough time to stand back and see the big picture.

When he gets back on the bus , he usually has reporters from the local papers on board - a few minutes each with the Candidate. Always in the back of his mind is the need to get on with the next big speech.

The bus pulls into the forecourt of a provincial hotel, a Thistle or a Holiday Inn. The manager is honoured to have him there. Hands are shaken. Someone is holding the lift door open. Tony and Cherie and staff go up to their rooms, a suite for the Blairs and another for the staff, who immediately set up office and grab a

Far left: Tony Blair onstage during a speech and (above) offstage before an appearance.

sandwich. Nobody has had time for lunch.

Always, the phones are ringing and there are more interviews to be done; the local and the national papers to be satisfied one by one. Sometimes a national newspaper political editor picks up the ringing phone on his desk to be told he's being put through to Tony and, without notice, is given ten minutes to do the interview he's been queueing for. Every minute of the Candidate's time has to be used.

In the provincial hotel, Alastair Campbell comes and goes from suite to suite, always phoning. He is more than a press secretary. He is a travelling campaign manager, screening the Candidate from decisions and callers he need not be bothered with. Anji Hunter, a sort of chief executive of Blair plc, sits cross-legged on the floor in her smart suit, phoning instructions about times and places and interviews for the hours ahead. If only the Tories could kidnap Anji, the Blair victory bandwagon might be stopped.

Now Tony wants an hour to write his speech. He takes off his tie and his shoes. He claps his hands and waves everyone out: "Come on, guys,

I've a speech to write". He sits with a couple of blank sheets. Tonight he will speak without notes, so he has to be specially well prepared. He is good with words. He has no fear of drying up. Those who watch him regularly are slightly awed by his ability to speak in perfectly-formed, grammatically correct sentences for half an hour or more. His only concern is that few credit him with conviction. That is why he has taken to speaking unscripted, so they can see it comes from deep within. Cynicism has to be fought at every campaign stop.

Quickly, the hour for preparation is gone. The staff are anxious about time for the journey to the leisure centre he's to speak in. He puts on his tie and shoes and jacket, the Candidate's uniform. He paces the corridor while someone calls and holds the lift. He's pacing in the same way he does on stage, the shape of the speech running round and round in his head. He is so intense that when his wife and his staff chatter in the lift, he doesn't hear them. He is listening to the speech. He has the look on his face that he has on stage, the leadership look.

January 27
PRE-ELECTION
TENSION

THE car park of the Bernard Arms, a country pub on the A4010 near Princes Risborough in Bucks, was unusually crowded for a Monday afternoon in January. Among the cars stood television vans. Inside, the saloon bar was packed, but curiously quiet. Everyone was listening to a slim young man sitting beside the slot machine, talking politics as people do in saloon bars.

He was being unusually complimentary about the Conservative government, highlighting the praise it deserved for creating "the strongest economy in Europe". He was a little biased though. The young man by the slot machine was the Secretary of State for Health, Stephen Dorrell. His note-taking audience of political journalists had gathered at the Bernard Arms, a couple of miles from Chequers, to be briefed on the Cabinet's election strategy meeting at the Prime Minister's country retreat.

The outlook facing the government that Monday afternoon was grim and nobody took Mr. Dorrell's upbeat briefing very seriously. For more than four years, the Conservatives had trailed Labour in the polls by more than 20 points. No governing party had ever been so far behind for so long. Each time the polls showed a slight recovery, the Conservatives fell back again. Every mistake they made - and they made plenty - was heavily punished by public opinion. What they got right counted for nothing. Mr. Dorrell may have been exaggerating when he talked of Europe's strongest economy, but by most measures the recovery was genuine and sustained. Yet the mounting evidence of national prosperity did the Conservatives no good. The country begrudged its ministers any credit for success. This was perhaps no more than they deserved, having taken no blame for recession. The government was into its last 100

> Some Tory MPs believed Major had resigned himself to going down. Far from being depressed, the certainty of defeat had released him from the cares of office.

days. The Conservatives' only hope was hope itself, their only strategy to hang on in case something turned up; preferably their poll rating. Michael Heseltine, the Deputy Prime Minister, had long argued in private that a year of rising living standards in the run-up to an election would always be enough to lift a government clear of its opponents. But the polling evidence could not be plainer - the economic recovery was not a rising tide that lifted all boats. The Tories were still sinking. Even while ministers were meeting at Chequers, MORI was conducting a poll for The Times which showed Labour's lead stretching by four points to 25. There was little at the Bernard Arms briefing to suggest that the Cabinet had done much more at Chequers than whistle to keep its spirits up.

Viscount Cranborne, Leader of the Lords, confided to colleagues that he had found the whole thing a waste of time. This would not have mattered so much had Major not asked Cranborne to be his chief of staff during the campaign. A Conservative spin doctor bravely quoted Nigel Lawson's dictum that "no government loses an election when the tide of ideas was flowing in its favour".

But there was no sign of even the merest trickle of ideas from Chequers that afternoon. The Cabinet, we were told, had discussed a tax-cutting agenda ... a grammar school in every town ... getting public spending below 40 per cent of national income ... appealing to the hard-working classes ... new initiatives on crime ... building a better Britain. The familiar phrases rolled up like bells and cherries on the slot machine beside Mr. Dorrell, though with little sign of a jackpot. Elinor Goodman, Political Editor of Channel Four News, summed it up brutally as she made for the car park and dialled her newsdesk by mobile phone: "There's **** all of a story here." The Conservatives had, for a whole afternoon, a captive audience of political editors and failed to plan a story that would dominate the evening news and morning papers. Could it be that they no longer had a story to tell the nation? The most striking image to emerge from Chequers was of John Major in a baggy jumper, unaware that it made him look a man taking a day off work to do some odd jobs around the place before handing over to new owners.

It had not been a good day for Her Majesty's Government. In the car back to London, the President of the Board of Trade felt sick. Ian Lang did not get back to the Commons to vote. The government lost by one. The defeat was the story that dominated the news, rather than images of a Cabinet fizzing with new ideas. In fact, the lost vote turned out to be a mistake. It had really been a tie. But a government whip, the hapless Tony Coombs, had miscounted. Luck, like the tide of ideas, was not running with the Conservatives.

Whatever the government tried, it seemed unable to stop making mistakes, like a batsman who loses form and can't help playing loose shots. Yet Major himself remained serene. He seemed to feel none of the turmoil and tension afflicting his party and indeed his opponents. Tony Blair looked more and more tightly wound, suffering as much as anyone from a malady which Speaker Betty Boothroyd diagnosed as "pre-election tension". Blair had a

problem familiar to any sports fan whose team has ever built up a lead and fretted through the closing stages of a game. Major had the advantage - his only advantage - of knowing he had nothing now to lose because the contest had been lost long ago.

Some Tory MPs believed Major had resigned himself to going down. Far from being depressed by it, the certainty of defeat had released him from the cares of his thankless office. As one shrewd Tory said: "He will probably campaign all the more effectively for having already accepted his end. And, after all, he can be pleased with surviving so long - not many Prime Ministers last six years."

Certainly Major was more at ease with himself than at any time since his early days as Prime Minister. He took to holding one-man press conferences without the word Conservative on the platform, as if to show that he stood above and apart from his wretchedly divided party. But still he needed some themes, if not a tide of ideas then at least a story to tell the voters. What emerged from the Chequers summit during the next few days did not encourage Tory optimism. The Sunday papers got hold of a wonderful story that several ministers had fallen asleep during the strategy session, having eaten too much plum crumble and bread and butter pudding for lunch. Who could deny them this last chance to tuck in? The next time the Cabinet gathered at Chequers it would surely be hosted by Tony Blair.

February 19
THE WIRRAL

BLAIR smiled as his car came off the motorway into Runcorn, on the way home from a day's campaigning in the Wirral by-election. Runcorn always makes him smile ruefully. He tells a story of canvassing there many years ago with a survivor of the last Labour Cabinet. The two of them spent 45 minutes at one house, before a frustrated Blair discovered the man they were persuading to vote Labour was the local Party chairman. The young Blair asked his eminent fellow canvasser what precisely they were doing to reach the voters who were not supporting Labour. "I don't know," came the reply. "What do you suggest?"

Blair had had nearly three years as Labour leader to answer that question, which the whole party was implicitly asking when it elected him in the numbing aftermath of John Smith's death. His entire leadership could be seen as a series of replies to that question: "What do you suggest?"

In his acceptance speech on the day he won the leadership, Blair said: "It is the confident who can change and the doubters who hesitate." Nobody doubted Blair's confidence, nor his appetite for change; they were not given time to. No leader, not even Margaret Thatcher, had ever blown through a political party with such whirlwind determination to change it.

Blair, who deeply respected Smith but was sometimes impatient with him, came to office full of pent-up energy. He had spent his entire political career in Opposition and hated the futility of it. A few days before his election as leader, Blair sat in the sunshine on the terrace at the back of the poky office he used as Shadow Home Secretary and said: "I can't hope to replace the trust and affection in which the country held John. I'm too young for that. I have to be something different. I have to be bold and exciting."

This was an understatement. The boldness and excitement of the Blair years have been well-

The young Blair asked his fellow canvasser what they were doing to reach voters who were not supporting Labour. "I don't know," he said. "What do you suggest?"

chronicled: abolishing Clause Four, building a mass membership to replace dominance by the block vote, rooting out vote-losing policies in a cultural revolution that climaxed in the pledge not to raise income tax. The Tories were disorientated by his speed of movement. They could never tell where his next ambush was coming from, nor work out where he would be off to next as they tried to counter-attack. Nor could his opponents within the party.

His boldness had disadvantages, though. The most dangerous was the risk that any leader runs when he changes his party - the suspicion that he stands for nothing except winning power. Curiously, nobody ever levelled this charge at that great conviction politician Margaret Thatcher, who turned herself and her party through 180 degrees on Europe, monetarism and grammar schools, to name but three.

It was hard to accuse Blair of inconsistency because he had, unlike Neil Kinnock, never been a leading advocate of the policies he was ditching. The speed of his rise gave him that advantage. The Tories made the best use of a quote from Blair's 1983 election address when, trying to get into parliament, he had naively backed the official policy of pulling out of Europe. Was this rookie candidate, selected at the last minute, supposed to have single-handedly stood up to the party leadership and repudiated its policy? No matter; the charge of saying anything to get elected was relentlessly made by the Tories, with some connivance from those Blair rolled over in the Labour Party.

His youthful enthusiasm, symbolised by his broad smile, helped substantiate the case against him. The more he changed the party, the more his enemies within and without questioned his sincerity and depth of political character. Yet Blair's outlook was not so different from Clem Attlee's. It angers Blair that anyone should question Labour's right to stand as the party of aspiration. He represents a Durham constituency and, as he often says, the Durham miners did not vote for Attlee in 1945 so that their sons could go down the pit. They voted Labour because they believed it was the party that would offer their sons a way out of the coalmines.

He could never understand how Labour had been so foolish as to mislay that appeal and let the Tories sneak off with it. To Blair, Labour's mistake was to allow itself to become exclusively the party of the underdog, a party apparently hostile to people who got on in life. He wanted Labour to once again represent both the underdog and the successful, against the privileged few - "the many, not the few", as he put it in his new Clause Four.

I remember having lunch with him a few days after John Major gave an interview in which the Conservative leader said that 15 per cent of our children get an excellent education, but the other 85 per cent, sadly, don't. Major was clumsily trying to say that he wanted to raise standards for the other 85 per cent. "We've got to be the party of the 85 per cent," said Blair. This was not so far from Attlee, who said during the 1945 campaign: "The Labour Party is , in fact, the one party which most nearly reflects in its representation and composition all the main streams which flow into the great river of our national life."

In a speech on the 50th anniversary of the 1945 victory, Blair said he wanted Labour to be the party of "the self-employed and the unemployed, small businesspeople and their customers, managers and workers, homeowners and council tenants, skilled engineers as well as skilled doctors and teachers." Blair, unlike most politicians who say such things, had no illusions about the harsh choices his words imposed. Customers, managers and homeowners may tell the pollsters they wanted higher government spending and did not mind paying more tax. They may claim to regard the defeat of unemployment as the number one priority. But in four elections running they had refused to take risks with their wellbeing by voting Labour. They had refused to gamble on Labour's good intentions. So Labour had to kick the habit of promising more government spending on every problem facing the country, because these people knew they would be paying the bills.

Blair once told me he would ideally like to see Labour have no spending commitments at all. John Smith had ordered his Shadow Cabinet to resist all temptation to make spending pledges, but the tough decisions lay ahead when he died. It was easy enough for shadow ministers to pay lip service to this new discipline. Few had thought it through to its conclusions. Blair had. At the start of election year, he sat down in the front room of his Islington home and came to an agreement with Gordon Brown that if Labour was credibly to promise no extra income tax, it must also promise no extra spending that could not be found from savings - for instance, more primary school teachers to be paid for by phasing out the assisted places scheme. This meant accepting the spending totals set out by Kenneth Clarke in what Labour hoped would be the last Tory budget. This was a harsh discipline indeed, after so many years of knee-jerk Labour condemnation of Tory cash cuts. But it was the price Labour had to pay if it wanted doctors, engineers and small businesses to have no fear of Labour.

The Wirral South by-election was a perfectly designed laboratory test of this aim. It had more homeowners, more two-car families, more managers, more golf courses than the national average. And it still had grammar schools. David Blunkett took the precaution of restating Labour's pledge that local authorities would not be free to abolish grammars. Blair was convinced, as he hustled through a morning in the constituency, that he had achieved his aim of killing the fear factor.

Though an admirer and friend of Neil Kinnock, he had no illusions about the country's fear of waking up and finding Kinnock in Number Ten. With the election now at most ten weeks away, Blair believed the most potent fear in people's minds was not of Labour, but of waking up and finding Major and his divided crew back in power. The by-election polls were as encouraging as the general election polls. The constituency, like the country, wanted the Conservatives out. Blair was determined there must be nothing to distract the voters from fearing a divided government that had presided over two recessions and broken its tax promises.

He judged people by the way they looked at him and he didn't see fear in their eyes. Kinnock

The Leader: Tony Blair   *The Deputy: John Prescott*

had memorably said that in the last days of the 1992 campaign he had noticed people looking away and had known they weren't going to vote for him. That had not happened to Blair - "so far," he said, ever wary of complacency. Blair had said from the beginning that he would "wage war on complacency". But he was finding the battle harder to fight. He no longer talked like a man who knew it might easily slip away from him if he failed to take care. There was too much evidence all around, in the boarded up shops and the cheers of the workers at the fridge factory and the warm welcome from their bosses, that the country really wanted a change. It looked and felt as though Blair had successfully answered the question the party had put to him - what do you suggest?

He seemed, as he was driven from the Wirral to Runcorn station, pretty convinced that he was going to win - not just the by-election, but on May 1. He had heard the Tory saying that Labour's support was a mile wide but a yard deep. However, he felt Labour support was hardening. He said one candidate had surveyed 900 "switchers" (ex-Tories coming over to Labour) a year ago and just gone back to question them again: 899 were still intent on voting Labour. The party's private polling suggested the Don't Knows were making up their minds at last and dividing half and half between Labour and the Tories - enough, said Blair. He agreed that there was always a danger of the economy pulling the Tories out of trouble, but he saw no sign of that happening. He didn't get the feeling that people believed things were as good as the Tories claimed. And, anyway, people weren't prepared to give the Tories credit for anything. They regarded them as a shower.

He was quite happy if Major wanted to play it long and go for May 1. This gave Labour more time to reassure people. For all the work he had done, all the toes trodden on and the egos bruised and the sacred cows led to the slaughter, Blair knew how much he still had to do in the campaign. The previous week, Labour had got together a focus group in Watford; that is, a group of voters who were regularly questioned so that their attitudes and the party's impact could be carefully tracked. Not one voter at this meeting had heard of Labour's pledge to hold down income tax. For all the agony behind that landmark decision, it had not registered.

The election was certainly not won yet, however straight people were looking into Blair's eyes. Far from being like a team that is winning with ten minutes to go and wants the whistle to blow, Labour was like the much-fancied favourites tensely awaiting kick-off. And there had been plenty of surprise cup results this season. During that car ride out of the Wirral, Blair confided his minimum target for by-election victory, on condition the figure didn't appear before the result. He wanted to win by 3,000 to be sure Labour was on course for power. At 1.30am on March 1, the result was declared. Labour had won by 8,000, a swing of 17 per cent. The Conservatives quoted previous by-election losses, but none had been so close to a general election. Never had a government surrendered a seat to the main Opposition on such a swing with so little time in which to recover.

IT'S hard to believe," said a Labour frontbencher, "but eight weeks from today I'm going to be sitting at home waiting for Tony to call from Number Ten." On a sunny March morning in Inverness, the Scottish Labour Conference was gathering to hear Tony Blair in a mood of high anticipation, mixed with a wary disbelief and, in some quarters, suspicion. Much of the Scottish Labour Party had never liked Blair. Its executive was described by one Blair ally in the Scottish party as "the last remaining unreformed outpost of old Labour". But even this critical audience could not help being infected by the excitement of impending victory. Veterans of successive defeats struggled to resist fate-tempting complacency. Shadow ministers seared by repeated disappointment forced themselves to wonder if things could really be going this well.

Another frontbencher, trying his best to remain pessimistic, said: "Don't forget that we haven't won an election since I joined this party." He could not help saying it with a grin. That morning's Daily Telegraph reported an 11-point leap in Labour's Gallup lead; at 26 per cent, it was twice as long as Attlee's lead over Churchill in 1945. A third of the remaining Conservative supporters said they "wouldn't mind" a Labour government.

It was not hard to see why. It had been a week to try the patience of the most loyal Tory, a week of calamities which typified the various reasons for approaching Tory defeat. First, Stephen Dorrell said the government would not be taking Britain into a single currency. After a telephone conversation with the Chancellor, Dorrell issued a "clarification" saying that government policy was unchanged. This was the second time in a fortnight that Ken Clarke had been obliged to ask a colleague to issue a statement supporting government policy. The Cabinet was becoming very careless.

> Barbara Castle paid tribute to his killer instinct. "Something we have needed for a long time. Someone who can fight the buggers on their own terms".

The whole party was too. A tape of rightwing backbencher David Evans talking like a caricature of Alf Garnett found its way on to ITN's 5.40pm bulletin, having been leaked by Labour to Evans' regional TV station. Evans said Virginia Bottomley was "dead from the neck up" and women like her got on in politics purely because they were women. He described his opponent in marginal Welwyn Hatfield as an unmarried mother with "three bastard children". Evans, a self-appointed tribune of Thatcher's people, had always been deliberately obnoxious, but as an elected member of the 1922 executive (the Tory backbenchers' shop stewards committee) he could hardly be dismissed as unrepresentative.

When poor Mrs. Bottomley went through a series of unconvincing TV interviews chirpily insisting that she accepted Evans' hollow apology, the impression was confirmed of a government for whom no indignity was too much. And then came the latest Douglas Hogg disaster. It emerged that a report on unhealthy conditions in abattoirs had lain unpublished for a year. Coming on the first anniversary of the BSE controversy, this new scandal revived public unease over food safety and, with it, the familiar charges of ministerial neglect, incompetence and secrecy.

The Prime Minister , uncomfortable in the face of Tony Blair's Commons questioning, claimed there had been no need to publish the damning report. His assurances carried as much conviction as Mrs. Bottomley's forgiveness of David Evans. Meanwhile the hapless Mr. Hogg , who had broken his foot falling down stairs at home, was pictured on all the bulletins hobbling about on crutches. It was an image that summed up the plight of a crippled government, limping to its end. Labour's only problem seemed to be over-confidence. At a celebration of Tribune's 60th birthday, Robin Cook talked of Labour winning "its second landslide this century". His exuberance was understandable in the context of an excitably crowded Covent Garden party, where Old Labour sounded as impatient for power as those Shadow Cabinet members deemed left-wing enough to attend such an event.

Michael Foot said Tony Blair's government was going to be as great as Attlee's. Blair was not present, but his name was cheered. Barbara Castle, casting aside her battle with Blair on pensions policy, paid tribute to his "killer instinct, something we've needed for a long time - someone who can fight the buggers on their own terms." Blair was not pleased by Robin Cook's talk of a landslide. The Labour leader was both superstitious and tactically wary of taking the result for granted. As he said in a memo to the Shadow Cabinet, Labour had not bettered a 3.2 per cent swing since Attlee; 4.1 per cent was needed now. "We have a mountain to climb," he warned. Labour could not afford wavering voters deciding to back the Tories in order to limit Labour's supposed majority; if too many took that view, there might not be any majority. The Labour leader wrote a passage of caution into his Inverness speech: "We are doing well. But we take nothing for granted ... even if we win, there will be no victory dances."

What he feared was a mistake like the Sheffield rally in 1992, when many voters were repelled by Neil Kinnock's apparent over-confidence on the election eve. At Inverness, Blair delivered his speech quietly, conversationally. It sounded as though he wanted to win without raising his voice. This was not the same thing as avoiding radicalism. Indeed, the significance of the Inverness speech was a long impromptu passage at the end of which Blair challenged the fashionable belief - widely held in this audience - that his government was so scared of the middle classes that it would make little difference. "Have a bit of faith," he asked. There was a hint of frustration in his off-the-cuff peroration, as if he was perturbed that his own party seemed not to have quite grasped the scale and purpose of what he wanted to achieve.

He tried to explain himself by referring to his father Leo, who had been a Conservative. "He wanted to get on and do well and he believed that if you do you have to become a Tory. That's rubbish. We want people to be prosperous and have money in their pockets. The difference is that we want everyone to do it." The people now coming over to Labour had always want to succeed "if only we would let them, if only we would say - we're not going to hold you back." When the Labour Party was formed it was "the party of real aspiration and ambition". Labour was formed "for reasons that are as valid today as they ever were". This earned him a standing ovation. Though some members of the Scottish executive looked unthrilled by Blair's appeal, it felt like more than a dutiful ovation. There seemed to be a longing in the applause - a longing to make it all come true, to win power and to make a difference.

But that feeling was not unanimous. "No vision," muttered one delegate to a comrade in the gents. "Or are we just a pair of dinosaurs?" Blair left town promptly. Shortly after he had gone, the results of the elections to the Scottish executive were announced. Seven anti-Blairites had lost their seats, giving control to the modernisers. The last Old Labour outpost had fallen; now for the electorate.

Back at Westminster, Tory Party sources were confiding that this was supposed to have been the week of the great fightback, but its centre-piece, the Prime Minister's announcement of a new private pensions policy, had been overwhelmed by the Dorrell, Evans and Hogg disasters. The next morning's papers carried pictures of Mr. Major unsuccessfully trying to unveil a plaque. The curtain refused to open, then came away from the wall in the Prime Minister's hands. Major did not know that at that moment Sir George Gardiner, the recently de-selected Tory MP, was finalising details of his defection to the Referendum Party, embargoed for the Sunday Times and Express, for whom he wrote viciously well-turned pieces on Major's poor leadership . The final curtain was surely not far away.

THE Conservative Central Council is a small-scale, spring version of the party conference, a select gathering of rock solid Tories. If the Conservative Party were ever to die out, these are the people who would be the last Tories standing. As they gathered in Bath on March 14th, it was not entirely fanciful to think of them as the last Conservatives. The party's poll rating was still falling and now time had run out. John Major had always regarded his Central Council speech as the probable launch of his campaign, but had always pictured himself arriving at this point with the polls at last turning in his favour; if not ahead, then coming strongly from behind. It hadn't happened and the electoral clock could be ignored no longer. Major was going to have to go into the election further behind than any Prime Minister before, still falling further back.

All week there were rumours that he was about to make a formal announcement, ahead of his Bath launch, and the broadcasters had their cameras ready at Buckingham Palace. But, typically, another disaster intervened; another leak prompting new fears about food hygiene. Douglas Hogg was forced to limp into the Commons to make an emergency statement on the afternoon of Wednesday, March 12 - hardly the backdrop for announcing an election. The following day would be the anniversary of the Dunblane massacre, a deeply unsuitable moment for the opening of party hostilities, so a Thursday announcement was out too. The suspension of party politics for the day - Major and Blair used Prime Minister's Questions to offer the nation's sympathy - created a vacuum.

Politics abhors a vacuum and this one was filled by Margaret Thatcher. There had long been talk of Thatcher saying at dinner parties that she was impressed by Tony Blair. Now a story surfaced that she had told the editor of The Times, Peter Stothard, that Blair "won't let Britain down". She could not have chosen four better

Major unveiled his campaign slogan: "You can only be sure with the Conservatives". It drew no applause.

words if she had tried; this was precisely the gut feeling Blair wanted wavering Tory voters to have. He did not expect them to enthuse over his programme, but he did want them feeling he would not be a risk. For someone who had never held office, there could not be a better endorsement of his basic soundness as a leader than Thatcher's. Blair and his advisors had been pondering how strongly to push the likeness between his firm leadership and hers, in contrast to Major's. Now the job had been done for them, for free. It was not the send-off Major needed for his big speech. The venue was the Bath Forum; from the outside a solid, handsome and enduring piece of English architecture, but inside as faded as an old cinema doomed to closure. The symbolism was irresistible to anyone going behind the facade, along the paint-peeling corridors to the Conservative Party's temporary command centre. The Forum was the perfect setting for the last gathering this century of the Conservatives as a party of power, a party whose enduring solidity had crumbled from the inside.

Putting the best face on a grim prospect, Conservative spin doctors explained to political correspondents that there were three important things to remember: elections are won by governments when (1) they deliver economic success (2) they win the battle of ideas and (3) there is no enthusiasm for the Opposition. All three conditions for a Tory victory were in place. "The Labour lead defies the laws of political gravity," according to Danny Finkelstein, the bright young former SDP man who was now head of Tory research.

There was something in each of Finkelstein's propositions - the economic indicators were looking good, Labour had indeed accepted much of what the Tories had put in place since 1979 and the polls did suggest people wanted the Tories out more avidly than they wanted Labour in. But the Finkelstein theorem was incomplete. Parties lose elections when they are (4) divided (5) led weakly and (6) gripped by a death wish. As if to demonstrate that (4), (5) and (6) all applied to the Conservative Party, Edwina Currie and John Biffen went on the BBC's World At One to discuss the prospects for defeat.

Mr. Biffen, a former Leader of the Commons, speculated that the landslide might be so dramatic that the leadership election may have to await by-elections for contenders who lost their seats. Mrs. Currie pleaded with John Major to go quickly if beaten: "Please, John, please don't hang around." This Friday lunchtime disaster was the kind of nasty accident that happens to divided parties whose senior members know they are heading for defeat and have scant respect for their leader's authority. Mrs. Currie may have had a long record of speaking too freely for her own good, but as an MP with a small majority she had no illusions about her leader's chances of delivering victory. She realised immediately how much damage she had done. When Michael Brunson, ITN's Political Editor, rang for a matching interview, she told him to "f*** off". He told her it was the only story than anyone was interested in at Bath. She said she didn't "give a f***".

Brian Mawhinney certainly did. The Tory chairman's speech included a vain warning to all Conservatives to say nothing if they could not say something that contributed to victory. The line was delivered with heavy menaces, but there was little Mawhinney could do against factors (4), (5) and (6). The Conservatives tried to turn the story round with an unusually copious briefing on what Major would say the next morning, but another self-inflicted disaster had set back the long-awaited Conservative counter-attack by another precious day. It was Currie, not Major, who dominated the news. According to the advanced billing, Major would be making an "intensely personal speech" to which he had himself devoted many hours of work. It would be about his passionate beliefs. The activists who assembled to hear it gave a strong impression of advanced age. The feeling of pensioners going to watch a black-and-white movie at a condemned cinema was heightened by the warm-up for Major - a short film on past triumphs.

The audience cheered the 1992 pre-election headlines predicting defeat and cheered even more loudly the clips of Major on his soapbox and Major waving to the crowd that gathered outside party HQ as victory was declared. They hissed at

a picture of Tony Blair; perhaps it was the imagination, but there seemed to be a frisson of fear when the Labour leader came up on screen. Then the lights went up and, instead of usherettes, out came Mr. and Mrs. Major. They took their ovation and then Norma left her husband alone on stage. There was no sign of the divided Cabinet. The lights dimmed again, leaving the spotlight on the lone Major. "Let me tell you about the next Queen's Speech," he said quietly. There would be an Education Bill that would abolish the assisted places scheme, a Bill that would begin the break-up of Britain ... For a moment it seemed that Major was about to speak the innermost fears of the party and concede the probability of a Labour victory, if only to scare the voters into line. But , no, the busy lighting technicians threw their switches again and in a warm blue glue, Major said: "Don't worry, that Queen's Speech will never be delivered." Instead, he would be back in power. "I am not asking you to vote for a Conservative Party led by Tom, Dick or Harry, but by me." This swipe at the manoeuvring Michaels and Stephens and Johns who hoped to succeed him was not in his text.

Getting down to the speech he had spent hours working on, Major unveiled his campaign slogan: "You can only be sure with the Conservatives." It drew no applause. "Our real opponent is more formidable than Labour," he said. "We're fighting the argument that it's time for a change". This drew a groan of weary familiarity. Against this menacing cliché, Major offered the well-worn counter argument: "We must not throw it away"; it being the strongest economy "since many years before the war". But the Bath speech was about more than the government's claimed economic success. Having failed to turn the polls by talking up the economy, Major had decided he must present himself as a man with a vision. "I dream of a people's Britain," he said. He wanted "to see the have-nots become the haves." His vision was not just for the lucky, the fortunate, the able, the self-confident. "It's for everyone, for those for whom life is a struggle, for those who don't have the best education, don't have a decent home, don't have a safe neighbourhood, don't have a job." This whole passage might have been lifted from a Tony Blair speech, indeed from any Labour politician past or present.

Major was trying to persuade the people that

he knew more about the struggles of real life than his public school opponent - an echo of his "New Labour, Old School Tie" crack at the party conference. Brixton Boy was clearly going to have a star role in the election. Major said he knew about people whose life was a struggle. "I come from them. I care for them and I long to see them have some of the finer things of life ... We're out to make sure that those who don't have, do have." This was a grand ambition - "it is what I have always longed to do." Six years into his premiership, it seemed a strange time to be revealing what he had always longed to do. It was, of course, a reprise of his early slogans, a classless society and a country at ease with himself.

Throughout his time in office, Major had periodically slipped into Brixton mode, talking not just the language of One Nation Conservatism, but of Social Democracy. Was this the real Major, or merely one of the many outfits used by a master of political disguise? He was now one of the longest serving Prime Ministers of the century, yet his party and his country could still not be sure who or what he was. He had come to office promising to put Britain at the heart of Europe, yet had later described himself as the biggest Euro-sceptic of them all. Thatcher had mistaken him for "One of Us", yet he had spent most of his leadership fighting a guerrilla war against her supporters. He had paraded his humble origins while serving and then leading a government which had deliberately reversed a century of increasing social equality. Now, sensing a national longing for a fairer society, he was trading on his ordinary-guy background, asking the country to believe that he was finally in a position to help the poor, having licked the economy into shape.

He did not mention why the economy had needed repairing, nor who had done the damage. This was meant as the speech of a man who knew how tough things had been. Even while mawkishly exploiting his early poverty, though, he made a telling slip; a jibe at John Prescott that jarred with his alleged feeling for the disadvantaged. It came in the course of a good joke about Labour's inexperience. Likening Blair's Cabinet to an airplane crew, Major mocked the newness of New Labour: "We're so new, none of us have flown before." He went on: "During the flight, our bar steward, John Prescott, will be coming

through the cabin." This was a reference to Prescott's time as a steward on an ocean liner. No Prescott profile was complete without mentioning how the Tory MP, Nicholas Soames, liked to call across the Commons at the deputy Labour leader: "Mine's a G & T , Giovanni." It was one thing for Soames to make this joke. He had shrewdly built a career for himself as a caricature High Tory. At 17 stone he looked the part of the well-fed grandee. As Churchill's grandson, he had pedigree. In the modern Tory Party of suburban salesmen, he was much-loved as the real thing: Good old Nick, doesn't give a damn. But beneath the Wodehouse buffoonery, there was a serious politician, who gloried in inequality as much as Thatcher had. Though fiercely loyal to Major - as a soldier he valued loyalty above all virtues except courage - Soames deplored the Prime Minister's guff about a classless society. He could be very amusing on the subject over lunch.

Now here was Major, anything but a grandee, apeing Soames's Prescott put-down in a speech purporting to show his concern for those who struggled in life. It was not the first time Major had sneered at Prescott. In his Bournemouth conference speech the previous autumn he had poked fun at Prescott's legendary looseness with the English language. Given that Major was portraying himself as a man who cared for those who had to fight for what they got out of life, his Prescott jibes sounded mighty close to snobbery. They were the kind of jokes the grammar school boy makes at the expense of boy who fails his 11-plus, as Prescott had. This was a strange thing for the champion of the classless society to do; but not perhaps so strange from a man who had chosen "a grammar school in every town" as a flagship election policy. This conflict between the classless Brixton Boy and the grammar school snob was only one of many contradictions in a character who was either extremely complex or simply a chameleon who changed his character not just from day to day, but moment to moment. Major's Prescott joke pleased his Bath audience; his Brixton Boy passages were meant for a public preparing to vote Labour. After the obligatory rendition of "Land of Hope and Glory", Major's people briefed that he would be going to the Palace on Monday.

PASSENGERS on the 1522 train from Swindon to Gloucester looked puzzled and slightly embarrassed, not liking to stare. Surely that was Tony Blair sitting with that nice-looking lady in a cream suit. Indeed, it was.

The Labour leader and his wife Cherie were on their way to one of the seats that would decide the election. Two or three of the bolder travellers, having done a double-take, came up and shook the Tony Blair by the hand and wished him well. One asked permission to take his picture. Another explained that she would not be able to vote Labour because she would be away. The candidate took the trouble to ask where she was taking her holiday; such a polite young man.

In 44 days, Tony Blair would almost certainly be Prime Minister, yet here he was, on a train, too humble to have a first-class compartment, travelling without security and minimal staff support. It was a strikingly democratic, down-to-earth way for the election favourite to start his campaign: making his way across the country he would soon be running in the same way as the people he would soon be leading.

There was nothing contrived about his choice of transport. The train from Paddington, with a change at Swindon, was the best way to get to the 58th seat on Labour's target list. If Gloucester were to fall, Labour would have achieved the swing it needed for a majority, so it was the obvious place to start the campaign. At last the election was under way. "Now it's for real," said Blair.

It had become real at 12.35pm, when Major came out of Number Ten to confirm that polling day would be May 1. Blair, at that moment visiting a school in south London, listened down a line arranged by ITN. Major said there had been a "dramatic change in the lifestyle of the people

"We're not going to spend the election preaching to the converted". This had always been their philosophy and was about to get its reward: the endorsement of The Sun

of this country". Labour had opposed everything the government had done and it would be "ironic" if they were to win - a curiously mild choice of word for a man launching the fight of his life. He thought it would be "very agreeable" to push Labour beyond soundbites. "I believe this election is winnable and I think I am going to win this election".

Was there not a slight feeling of going through the motions in Major's flat rhetoric? Blair looked eager and excited, perhaps relieved too, in his live TV interviews that followed the announcement. On the train to Gloucester, he had the air of an athlete who has brought himself to a peak of fitness for the race of a lifetime, knows he could not be in better condition and feels he is in prime form. "I've prepared for this for a long time," he said. He was surprisingly relaxed. Though his staff said he had lots of work to do, he had plenty of time to chat, enjoy the journey and savour the moment. Looking out of the train window somewhere in Gloucestershire, he pointed out a lovely view of houses on a wooded hillside - "isn't that beautiful".

In his first newspaper interview of the campaign, for The Mirror, he struck a note of national pride, conscious that the challenger must beware of seeming to knock and sneer. "This is a great country and it needs a government to match up to it," said Blair. His campaign theme would be: "Britain deserves better." His children, he said, had asked at breakfast if the election was now on and what was going to happen. He had given them the same reply he had given everyone tempted to be carried away by Labour's poll lead: "Never take anything for granted in this life." He said the thing he feared most was complacency. He seemed unafraid of John Major's supposed campaigning skills ("let's wait and see") or the prospect of a long campaign in which the Tories would make him crack ("for three years they

have been trying that"). He did not regard the election as a personal fight against John Major. Indeed he thought one of Major's problems was that he seemed to regard Labour's challenge as "somehow against him personally".

This shrewd phrase offered a rare glimpse of Blair's view of his opponent. It suggested that Blair had grasped something often overlooked about Major: his thin-skinned tetchiness. It was a potential weakness if Labour could bring it to the surface, though Major was long-practised in the art of looking nice and harmless.

For all Blair's political skills and the cleverness of his party's chief propagandists, they had never quite managed to dent Major's nice-guy image. Even at this late stage they were looking hard for a key word or phrase or image that would unwrap the Honest John packaging. Blair himself, though, gave a strong impression, as the 15.22 rattled through the countryside, of feeling he had the measure of his opponent - without, of course, committing the unpardonable crime of complacency.

At Gloucester station, Tony and Cherie Blair were greeted by cheering party workers carrying red balloons. However, the Labour leader had come to see someone even more important than his supporters. He had come to meet voters who might be coming over from the Tories and Liberal Democrats. His first campaign engagement was with a gathering of 22 "switchers", as they are known in the political trade. It was a very different kind of campaigning from the time-wasting canvass in Runcorn that had frustrated Blair all those years ago. "We're not going to spend this election preaching to the converted," said Alastair Campbell. This had always been the Blair-Campbell philosophy and it was about to get its reward: the endorsement of The Sun. The paper "wot won it" - allegedly - for Major in 1992 had decided to back Blair's New Labour. It was like winning a weathervane marginal. A party that had traditionally had to fight most of the press as well as the Conservatives was going into the election with the country's two biggest papers, The Sun and Mirror, behind it.

Above: Tony Blair, John Prescott and a host of children launch Labour's poster campaign. Previous pages: Tony Blair campaigning.

JUST as a dying man is supposed to see his whole life flash before him, so John Major's dying government seemed doomed to have its whole wretched existence re-enacted fast-forward in the campaign.

Right at the start, it was obliged to re-live the galling experience of having potentially good news wiped out by bad. One reason for John Major announcing the election when he did was in order that the monthly jobs figures could be the first big campaign news. They were due out on Wednesday, so on Tuesday evening, Conservative newspapers were discreetly invited to speculate on a 50,000 fall in unemployment the following morning. This was a calculated under-estimate. The true figure, as leaked to The Mirror, was 68,000. But it did not dominate the news. Labour and the Liberal Democrats succeeded in pushing another issue to the top of the bulletins and on to the front pages - sleaze.

Sir Gordon Downey, the parliamentary watchdog appointed in response to the repeated sleaze controversies since 1992, was due to report any time on a tangle of allegations against ten MPs. The most notorious was Neil Hamilton, a former trade minister who had been forced to quit over accusations that he took money from the owner of Harrods, Mohammed Al-Fayed, in return for tabling questions. Cash-for-questions, which had first struck the government in 1994, was a story that would not go away. It stuck like tar, besmirching the Tory Party's good name. Along with tax rises, the pound's ejection from the ERM and divisions over Europe, the Hamilton saga had done as much as anything to undermine the government.

Now it emerged that Downey's report would be ready the following week. But, because Major had announced the pro-rogation of parliament

The Times colour piece was sceptical . . . noting that when Major was asked an aggressive question about privatisation his answer was drowned by the noise of a passing train

for this Friday, Downey would have no parliament to report to. His findings would remain unpublished until after the election. The two Opposition parties accused Major of deliberately shutting parliament down before this potentially damaging report came out. It was, indeed, strange that parliament was being prorogued within five days of the election announcement, but not dissolved for a further 18 days. Such a long gap was unusual, even taking account of Easter weekend. Whether Major had been too clever by half in his election timing, or had not been clever enough to spot the trouble ahead, the Downey report was the perfect issue for the Opposition parties.

The Liberal Democrats were the first to raise it - Simon Hughes was howled down at question time - but it was only when Labour's media machine went into over-drive that the issue over-ran every other campaign story.

The Tories frequently complain about the impact of Labour's so-called spin doctors and they were to cry foul now about the use of the Downey controversy to divert attention from the jobless figures. They were right to. It was a brilliant operation. David Hill, Labour's chief media spokesperson, worked hard to crank the story up on the Tuesday evening, playing on the journalistic instinct that news is something that someone somewhere wants hidden, as Lord Northcliffe once said.

Although the Tories were entitled to fear and loathe the Labour propaganda machine, it could not work in a vacuum. What the Conservatives could never understand was that the Labour spin doctors worked with the grain of journalistic feeling. There was something wrong with the way some Tory MPs had used their influence with government and it was in the blood of good reporters to find this a more fascinating topic than the trumpeting of official jobless figures.

David Hill, who was a spin doctor long before the term was thought of, has a better feel for the reporters' gut instincts than anyone in politics. There is no mystery about his skill. He spends hours walking up and down Burma Road, which is the political correspondents' nickname for the narrow corridor where most of them have their cramped offices. David Hill is constantly talking to and, more important, listening to political reporters about what is going on. There is never a quiver of controversy that Hill's sensitive nose does not sniff out on his daily travels. And nobody reacts more quickly or with a surer touch to the latest story. He has another, more critical, attribute. He is trustworthy. However hard he spins, nobody has ever doubted his word or his judgement. He has never sold a pup in his life.

The Conservatives have never had anyone to match him, though their intelligence operation improved after the recruitment of Sheila Gunn from The Times. Now, with the election called, she was seconded to Major's personal campaign.

David Hill's philosophy was that, with Labour so far ahead, the Tories needed to use every day to cut the deficit; they would need roughly a one point gain for every working day. Labour therefore must fight a daily guerrilla war to deny the Tories any victories. By wiping out the impact of the unemployment total, Labour had denied the Tories a day that would have been theirs. Better than that, the story ran right into the weekend. The Tories had lost a whole week.

It was a week in which every little thing went wrong for Major. His plan had been to exploit the initiative of the election-caller and get out and about as the man of the people, in the market squares, in the middle of the crowd. It was a reprise of his soap box strategy of 1992, when Major felt the country had responded to the sight of him facing up to the street corner hecklers.

As soon as he announced the date he headed for Luton, with his fabled box. But the papers mostly carried unimpressive pictures of the Prime Minister surrounded by Special Branch and Conservative Party minders. Next day he went to Woking for a photo-opportunity with racing driver David Coulthard. Major seemed to be working the Tory heartlands, like a man fighting to save what he could, in contrast to

Blair's deliberate choice in Gloucester of a seat he must win - the action of a man seeking victory among the unconverted.

The Times' colour piece on Major in Woking, by Arthur Leathley, was sceptical, portraying Norma as glum and noting that when Major was asked an aggressive question about rail privatisation his answer was drowned by the noise of a passing train. This was the last paragraph, yet the Prime Minister found time to read all the way to it and get angry; so angry that correspondents were briefed on his fury at the unfairness of the way he was being reported.

It is a strange thing about John Major that, for a man who gets such a bad press, he is addicted to reading it. He is a political masochist. Once, at an economic summit in Japan, I was told how angry he was at a weak single-paragraph joke I had made, likening him to Des O'Connor. When I expressed disbelief that he should have troubled to read such a trifle while attending an important summit so far from home, I was told that was in his nature.

John Major's tetchiness was given a rare public display at his last Question Time. Inevitably, Blair raised the sleaze inquiry. Major was entitled to respond robustly, but he went beyond that, smearing Blair by questioning the funding of his private office and resurrecting the dead controversy over a trip to America on Concorde, which had been investigated and found to be within the rules. Honest John seemed oddly unable to see a distinction between the funding of Blair's legitimate parliamentary activities and the persistent allegation that some Tory MPs had accepted bundles of notes for their personal accounts in return for tabling questions.

His impotent fury at the loss of the electoral initiative made for a compelling final question time. Major shouted back at Blair. When the Labour leader said the Conservatives were going out with a stain on their character, Major riposted that the stain was on the Opposition front bench. When Paddy Ashdown joined the attack, Major called him "pious and pompous".

It was not very dignified, not very Prime Ministerial. Throughout these exchanges , the obscure backbencher David Shaw barracked and bayed as if determined to embody the unhappily departing soul of the Tory government. The Speaker reprimanded him, but left the task of expelling him for bad behaviour to his constituents in Dover, the Tories' 15th most vulnerable seat.

Major made his way out of the chamber the moment question time ended. His MPs waved their order papers , the traditional form of parliamentary applause - inviting inevitable jokes about waving goodbye. Many of them had never sat on the Opposition benches, including Major himself.

Next morning, with the House prorogued, the PM visited Gatwick. The Conservatives cancelled plans to take a busload of political correspondents and instead took only invited news agency and television reporters. Major was furious with the national papers for, as a Conservative source put it, taking the Labour agenda hook, line and sinker. Tory HQ privately admitted the opening week had been, as one official said, "intensely disappointing". Major had hoped to use the long campaign to get Labour on the back foot, but had not succeeded yet.

The point of his Gatwick trip was to have him helicoptering above a logo on the ground, saying: "Britain is Booming, Don't Let Labour Blow it." This is what the Tories had wanted the opening week to be about. But the only story anyone cared about was the reaction to five pages of sleaze allegations in The Guardian. Mr. Major said the charges were "junk"; not very Prime Ministerial, very tetchy. The man who was watching his premiership flash by had once again seen good economic news wiped out by controversy over his party's ethical standards.

IT ISN'T over until the final whistle blows," Tony Blair told a teenage questioner who wanted to know if he thought he was going to win. Blair was in Aberdeen, visiting a school. Back in London, the Conservatives were proving his cautious adage right.

At last, they had got an anti-Labour issue running and Labour's fumbled response showed the game wasn't yet won. The issue was trade union power.

The man who got it running was the wily old pro, Michael Heseltine. There had been much controversy and concern in the Tory Party over the division of campaign power between Heseltine; Brian Mawhinney, the party chairman; and the PM's election "chief of staff", Viscount Cranborne. Who would be in charge while Major was on the road? There should never have been any doubt, since Heseltine had a virtual monopoly of this unbalanced trio's stock of talent and tactical nous. Heseltine is the supreme opportunist of modern politics. Blair always had wary respect, regarding Heseltine as a genuinely big hitter. He is a street fighter, not so thuggish as Mawhinney, but much more dangerous - a dandy wearing knuckle-dusters inside his white gloves. Nobody is a better judge of the well-aimed low blow than Heseltine.

He saw his opportunity when The Daily Telegraph led its front page on Monday, March 24, with a report that Labour would grant recognition rights where a majority of staff voted to belong to a union. This had long been Labour policy. Indeed, the cynic might say it was one of the few policies Blair had let stand. But this old story was skilfully presented as new on the grounds that the pledge would be included in the business manifesto planned by Blair and Gordon Brown, which Labour had spent the weekend talking up.

> This was a telling moment. Journalists are like dogs who can smell weakness. They will tear apart a politician who is not sure of himself. Blair was completely confident.

The elevation of this story into a Labour mini-crisis over the next 48 hours was a textbook case study of the way politics and the media feed on each other during a campaign. With the story leading a national daily, it was inevitable that Blair would be asked by the broadcasters for a response. He replied dismissively that such recognition rights existed in the United States, so they could hardly be called a threat to business. This answer was carried on the bulletins, ensuring that the issue reached a wider audience than the Telegraph's readership.

That might have been that, but the Daily Mail piled in next morning with an inspired follow-up: "63 Firms On Union Hit List".

This too led the front page. A beautifully crafted piece, it said 63 firms would be "dragooned" into recognising a union. They would in the vanguard of Labour plans to impose "compulsory" recognition. These two words had been carefully chosen for their emotive impact. People don't like being dragooned. Compulsion carried echoes of the old closed shop - most definitely not Blair policy - which had done so much to discredit trade unionism in the 1970s. The Mail's language gave the policy a more threatening air than if it were described as freedom from exploitation by employers who refuse to deal with unions even when a majority of their staff vote for recognition in a secret ballot.

The Mail's menacing story was irresistible to Heseltine. The Conservatives had scheduled a "positive" press conference on education with Gillian Shephard. That was scrapped and replaced by a session of blood-curdlingly negative campaigning on the return of union power.

In a vintage display of ham-actor horror, Heseltine said companies would become "battlegrounds", firms would be subject to "licensed industrial blackmail" and "incalculable damage" would be done to the economy. Nobody does this stuff better than Heseltine. The old pro's performance may have been preposterously over-the-top, but it unsettled Labour. And it ensured that union power dominated TV coverage of the election.

Thus the Conservative newspapers had turned a non-story into news and kickstarted the Tory campaign. This newspaper role, of unofficial scriptwriters for Conservative campaigns, has always been more valuable than backing the Tories in the - mostly un-read - leader columns. So much for Lord Rothermere saying, as he had only that weekend, that his papers might not endorse any party. They had no need to. The Daily Mail was doing a better job than the Conservatives themselves.

The Mail and the Telegraph were able to report the following day on Labour "disarray", as the party tried to finesse the problem by fleshing out its policies with safeguards. For the first time the Tories had pushed Labour on to the defensive, exploiting folk memories of the 1979 Winter of Discontent. Danny Finkelstein briefed that union power was even more feared by those who did not remember '79 than by those who did. It seemed that the dread went deep among those brought up on grim tales of life in that distant country, Britain before Thatcher.

All this happened while Blair was out of town. He went by train to Derbyshire and Sheffield on the Monday and by plane to Aberdeen on Tuesday. He was not completely out of touch, thanks to Alastair Campbell's mobile phone. But you can't take the political temperature down a phone line, or properly sense the mood of the media while dealing with a question and answer session with schoolchildren.

Blair does these visits well. Children are more to him than campaign props. He actually likes them. Watching him and Cherie gathering frogs with a group of youngsters who were studying the environment at a High Peak nature reserve, no cynic could doubt that Labour's first couple were enjoying themselves. It was, of course, a useful bonus that the pictures looked good and that the daily image of the Blairs among smiling young faces emphasised Labour's appeal as the party that cares about our children's future.

As Blair said over and over, the election was a choice between hope and fear. While he was

out and about, exuding hope, Heseltine was ruthlessly stoking ancient fears of Labour in power.

Back in London for a meeting on the manifesto, Blair badly needed to get a grip. John Major had always intended the long campaign to be a test of Labour's nerve and of Blair's ability to hold his party on course. The first test had now arrived. Blair was due to hold a press conference after the traditional joint meeting of the Shadow Cabinet and national executive to finalise the election platform. There was a danger of it being hijacked by the Tories' union-power agenda.

Blair refused to be hijacked. Rather than wait to be pushed on to the subject by hostile questioning, he tackled it head-on in his opening statement. The "Tory lie machine" would churn out many inventions about Labour during the campaign, so he just wanted to say this: "The unions will get fairness but no favours from us and anyone who thinks we have created today's Labour Party only to hand it over to the unions or anyone else does not know me and has not been listening to a word I have said these past three years. This is a party that will govern for all the people, the whole country - and no single interest group within it."

When the questions did come, he was even tougher. Flying pickets, strikes without ballots, unelected leaders - all that had "gone for good".

He understood why the Conservatives want to fight the 1997 election as if it were 1979. But: "I have not made all these changes just to go back to the past. There will be no going back to the past and there will be no favours for the trade unions".

Even with Labour's changes to trade union law, Britain would have "more restrictive union legislation than any country in the western world".

It was a command performance, brimful of confidence and brutally unlike anything any previous Labour leader would have said. It was a very personal statement. Blair was in fact saying: you don't really believe I'm going to let the unions push me round. He knew that nobody present did believe that because they had all watched him in action at close quarters. To judge from the lack of interest in further questioning on the union issue, it seemed that he had fully answered the questions raised by the

Tories, simply by offering his own character and record as an unanswerable case for the defence.

This was a telling moment. Journalists are like dogs, who can smell fear and weakness. When they do, they will not let go. They will tear apart a politician who is not sure of himself or his case. The best defence, as against a growling mutt, is self-confidence. But it cannot be faked. Blair, having routed his union opponents to Clause Four reform, was completely confident in his ability to stand up to them with an election mandate behind him. The issue was not union power, but Blair power. The main topic of the press conference only emphasised Blair's command. He had just pushed the manifesto through the joint meeting of Shadow Cabinet and national executive in record time, a mere 90 minutes. Only Dennis Skinner had tried to move any amendments and he couldn't find a seconder, even among the trade union representatives. As one shadow minister said: "It was such a contrast to those interminable sessions in 1987 and 1992".

The manifesto would not be published for another week, but Blair said it was the first from Labour to promise tax cuts. "Today marks the burial of tax and spend politics from Labour", he declared.

Only once was Blair for a moment thrown. Revealingly, it was by a question about Margaret Thatcher. Why had he said Britain needed a sense of direction after six years of weak leadership - did that imply admiration for John Major's predecessor?

Amused by his own hesitation, Blair grinned and said: "That's a good question. I don't think anyone would doubt that we had strong leadership in the 1980s, though I wouldn't agree with everything that was done."

His regard for Thatcher has often been misunderstood, sometimes mischievously. He deplores her divisive dogmatism and her disregard for the victims of her two-nation society. But he respects her consistency and self-belief. As he often says, he hopes to drive through education reform with all the determination she brought to trade union reform. Blair has the same view of Thatcher as the apocryphal Essex man, who is supposed to have said: "She may be an old cow, but she certainly knows how to run a country."

What makes Blair a dangerous politician is that he doesn't care where he gets good ideas from and doesn't mind taking them from opponents. Since the oldest good idea in politics is strong leadership, why let Thatcher keep the British patent?

Blair's response to Labour's current difficulty on union policy had been thoroughly Thatcherite; not ideologically - that afternoon the Lady did a "hands up" turn for the cameras depicting Blair as a man who had surrendered to the unions (so over-the-top that it made Heseltine look like Sir John Gielgud). Blair's approach was psychologically Thatcherite. Like her, he was more than a party leader. He was prepared to stand apart from his party when it suited him, as she often had. By making his strength the issue, as she used to, Blair had contained Labour's first potential crisis of the campaign.

The episode had served as a warning to Labour that the Tories were still in the game and could still play, despite being terribly far behind. And it had shown the best way for Labour to counter-attack under pressure: through their centre forward.

As one senior Labour figure said afterwards, with some relief: "Tony reminded us today why we elected him leader."

Blair had done something else. By hitting back hard, he had shown there were some things he believed in and wasn't going to ditch because they were awkward. The voters might be suspicious of Labour's union policy, but they like a leader who knows where his bottom line is. On that, Blair had not yet established himself as Thatcher-like in the public mind, so it did him no harm to draw his bottom line on the freedom of individuals to join a union.

Following page: With the White Cliffs of Dover as the backdrop, Tony Blair mentally surveys the future for Britain.

March 27
TO THE
SLAUGHTER

HE came out of the front door with his wife beside him and said: "I now believe it is in the best interests of my constituency association and the Conservative Party if I withdraw..."

Tim Smith was the latest in a long line of Tories to play out this grisly resignation scene during the unhappy life of the 1992-7 parliament. The scene had become so familiar as to have its own rituals - the initial defiance, the media siege, the hints from the high command that it was time to go, the glum statement before the cameras at the gate, the loyal wife, finally the relief among untainted Conservatives who were sure they could at last now turn to the business of restoring the party's good name.

The ritual went by the name of sleaze, a very British word that falls just short of corruption, of which we like to think ourselves incapable. The term had first entered the political language within weeks of John Major's election victory, when his friend David Mellor was caught by a Sunday newspaper having an affair with an actress. He held out for weeks in those far-off days when it was still a strange idea that a Sunday paper could bring down a senior minister with a story about his private life. Mellor set many aspects of the ritual in place, including the happy-family photo-opportunity designed to show that everyone was prepared to put an unfortunate incident behind them. He was the first to find that it was not as easy as that.

Another aspect of the ritual created by the Mellor affair was the sordid detail; each sleaze controversy had one of its own which lodged in the public mind and, sooner or later, did for the MP concerned. In Mellor's case the sordid detail that proved his undoing was the revelation that his lovemaking with Antonia de Sancha

> His resignation was meant to be the honourable thing, but the timing was unhelpful. Three days had gone by without sleaze dominating the news. Suddenly it was back.

involved the sucking of toes.

In Tim Smith's case, the sordid detail was the stuffing of used £50 notes into brown envelopes - so many of them that he couldn't recall precisely how much he had been paid. The public may have little interest in the intricate details of the controversy surrounding Smith and Neil Hamilton, the other MP besieged by allegations that he took cash for questions. But that image of notes in envelopes could be clearly understood and readily condemned.

Smith, like Hamilton, was under investigation by Sir Gordon Downey and the row over the delayed Downey report had dragged him blinking into the election spotlight. At first, it had looked as though his constituency association in Beaconsfield would stand by him, and so the story had petered out over the weekend. But Beaconsfield Tories were, in fact, deeply unhappy at the prospect of campaigning for their soiled sitting MP and Smith had now come to realise he must stand aside. So he went lamb-like to the ritual slaughter at his front gate.

His resignation was meant to be the honourable thing, but the timing was highly unhelpful to John Major. Three days had gone by without sleaze dominating the news. Suddenly it was back. Smith was top of the bulletins.

Smith was actually the second MP of the week to quit under pressure. Allan Stewart, a former Scottish Office minister, had very quickly stood down at Glasgow Eastwood, missing out much of the ritual, following a newspaper story that he had had an affair while under treatment at a clinic for alcoholics.

It couldn't get any worse for the Tories, could it? Well, yes, it could and promptly did. On News At Ten, Michael Brunson concluded his report on the Smith resignation by saying a fresh scandal was about to break over yet another MP in the next morning's press. Sure enough, Piers

Merchant was pictured kissing "a 17-year-old Soho night-club hostess". Her job-description was the ritual sordid detail in the Merchant affair.

John Major's government was not the first to suffer scandals. But, as with by-election defeats, no government before had suffered so many, nor had any endured its torment right up to the election. The ritual Tory sacrifices never achieved the aim of lifting the curse of sleaze.

So, once again, the issues, which all the parties kept saying they wanted to campaign on, were off the agenda.

In his Beckenham constituency, Merchant struck the ritual stance of defiance, posed for ritual pictures with his ritually loyal wife. And Michael Heseltine did the ritual high command job of menacingly hinting it would be better to quit. Merchant refused to take the hint. Major dropped another, but still Merchant refused to go.

Meanwhile, it was reported that the emergency services had been called to Allan Stewart's home and taken him to a psychiatric hospital. Conservative Central Office said the MP had suffered a breakdown under the stress of recent events. So had the Tory election campaign. John Major had, with a brief union-bashing lull, now lost both the extra weeks of campaigning he had given himself by playing it long. This was clearly disastrous for the Conservatives, who had failed to make the health of the economy the main talking point of the nation, or to put Blair under serious pressure. But were these Tory disasters, coming along in bunches like buses, entirely good for Labour?

Blair's bravura performance on union rights had been downgraded by the news bulletins because of Smith's resignation. The "end of the Piers show" wiped out a Labour press conference on the government's broken VAT pledge. Much as Major wanted to talk up his achievements, Labour needed to remind the voters of what Major had done wrong. It was Heseltine's First Law Of Elections that, if living standards rose for a year before polling day, people would forget whatever went before. Labour wanted to remind the public of the broken Tory tax promises that were now fading memories, but its campaign too was going unheard in the din from the Tory slaughterhouse.

The Easter weekend was as painful for the Conservative Party as a visit to the dentist. It was meant to be a relaxing break, with the leaders retiring to their constituencies for a last rest before the real campaign began. But the weekend was four days of torture for the Tory Party.

Hamilton and Merchant refused to be pulled from their seats. Worse still, another scandal broke. Sir Michael Hirst, chairman of the Scottish Conservatives, resigned in anticipation of a Sunday newspaper story about his private life. He was alleged to have had a gay affair with an assistant.

Hirst's prompt resignation seemed at first sight to be a straightforward case of a decent man doing the right thing. But it soon became clear that there was something murky behind the resignation, a scandal more damaging to the Tory Party than a gay relationship.

Sir Michael, it seemed, had been stitched up by his Tory opponents. Mickey Hirst had made enemies during the battle for control of the Scottish Tory Party in the early 1990s. His allies now accused his opponents of taking their revenge. The charge was that, hearing the papers were sniffing round his private life, they exaggerated the extent of the press's knowledge, even suggesting the existence of compromising pictures, which did not exist. In an emotional scene at Hirst's home, they forced him to resign, according to the version told by Hirst's allies.

> Major got the worst of both worlds. He seemed stuck with the two MPs and, by letting his sources talk tough, had merely advertised his impotence

Major wrote a fulsome letter to Mickey Hirst, commending his courage in standing down so quickly. Central office briefed that this was meant as a hint to Hamilton and Merchant that they should go. This briefing was a bad mistake. There is no point talking tough if you are not in a position to act tough - a point John Major never learned in his admittedly difficult time in charge of the Tory Party. Even while the high command was sending this unambiguous signal, the executive of the Beckenham party was gathering for a meeting which voted 43-3 to endorse Piers Merchant's candidature. Hamilton meanwhile had leaked his Downey inquiry evidence to the Sunday Telegraph, hoping this would help clear his name. "It's all out war," he said. Central office stepped up the pressure by hinting, off the record, that the two MPs might be forced out, either by having the whip withdrawn or by having their local parties disbanded.

This kind of talk is fine as long as you mean it. But, with Hamilton and Merchant digging in, the high command's briefing went into reverse. "We don't want Armageddon," said one source. So Major had got the worst of both worlds. He seemed stuck with the two MPs and, by letting his sources talk tough, had merely advertised his impotence. The Conservative Party could not have worked its way into a worse position from which to launch an election campaign if it had tried.

April 1 – 2
ON THE ROAD

IT HAD turned midday in Northampton market square. A small crowd has gathered. Some know what they are waiting for. Others , drawn by curiosity, are happy to hang about in the spring sunshine and see what turns up. Eventually a coach pulls in. It has blackened windows. The giveaway to its occupant's identity is the windscreen slogan: "New Labour, New Britain." The shoppers of Northampton are the first target of Tony Blair's election tour.

His staff pull a wooden box from the luggage hold. Is it a soapbox? No, it's the People's Platform, say Labour's spin doctors. Tony Blair is going to visit at least 60 towns before polling day and he will be down among the people, speaking off the cuff from his platform. They say

The great persuader emerges from the bus, bounces up on to his box and says, "Hello Northampton. It is a beautiful day. The sun is out and with your support the Tories will be out on May 1"

he's not interested in the soft option of packed party meetings. He is "the great persuader" and for the next month we are promised he will be out there finding wavering voters to persuade.

The great persuader emerges from the bus, bounces up on to his box and says: "Hello, Northampton. It's a beautiful day. The sun is out and, with your support, the Tories will be out on May 1."

This is a big moment for Tony Blair. There is no training course for Prime Ministers and no way of preparing to run for the highest office. Like all MPs, he has made thousands of speeches and shaken a million hands. But being the leading man is different. There is no knowing if you are up to it until you are there on stage, alone, the only one

Tony and Cherie Blair launch his battlebus and invite the nation to get on board Labour's campaign. Following page: Blair gives his first battlebus speech, in Northampton.

who can win it or blow it. This most demanding role has, by its nature, to be played unrehearsed. There is nowhere to practice but in public. Working an election crowd takes low skills that don't necessarily come in a package along with the others a leader needs - the high intellect and the broad vision, the animal cunning and the cold blood required to run a political party.

Blair has long proved himself as a party manager. He knows how to set the agenda, confuse the Conservatives and mesmerise the media. But how good is he with real people? Watching Blair perform in a market square is like seeing an operatic tenor doing a night-club turn. Belting it out is not his style.

But the shoppers cheer his pledges: "Smaller class sizes, re-building the NHS, jobs, skills and apprenticeships for our young people - they shouldn't be on the dole, they should be out doing

a decent job." These are the priorities he has chosen in his ruthlessly pared down programme and, whatever the polls say, he has to convince the uncommitted that his pledges count and can be delivered. They have been tested and re-tested with the focus groups. Now the whole country has become one big focus group.

He speaks for three minutes, promising not a revolution but a fresh start.

"Britain deserves better. Let's make sure Britain gets it."

He steps down from his box and, with Cherie, gets among the crowd. They handshake their way towards the candy floss stand and then back towards Burger King, before plunging in among the stalls. A woman who had brought her baby daughter into town for a routine day's shopping recovers from her surprise and, braving the camera scrum, offers up the child for the leader's first baby-kiss of the campaign.

Democracy has many strange rituals. After the baby-kiss, the would-be Prime Minister buys a bunch of bananas for 89p. The stallholder,

Steven Tedechi, confesses to being "a Major man, really".

Among the shoppers, 76-year-old Evelyn Mills says: "He seems a nice young man."

Julie Rowlands, 36, says: "He didn't seem too bad."

As Mr. Blair always says - every vote has to be earned, none is taken for granted.

Beyond the media ruck, the people of Northampton go about their business oblivious to the politician moving among them. Those who happen upon the slow-moving maul are mostly intrigued, though some are irritated by the intrusion of politics into their lives - surely the mood of the nation as a whole.

The edge of the crowd is a good place to monitor attitudes to Tony Blair, by listening for responses to the repeated question: "Who is it?"

"The next Prime Minister," a father tells his son. "It's Tony Blair," says a shopper who resents the obstruction in her path. "Bleeding ridiculous."

"It's a politician - keep moving," says a young woman to her friend. They make off, beyond reach of Blair's appeal, not knowing they are his real target - the don't-knows and the don't-cares, the people who think all politicians are liars, the reluctant masses who refuse to listen.

John Major needs them even more - at this moment he is seeking them at a garden centre in Croydon. If there are parts of the electorate the pollsters haven't reached, they are among these disenchanted people who might yet have an unpredictable impact on polling day if only they can be persuaded to use their vote.

The Blairs get back on their bus, with its side-window slogan: "Leading Britain". It is followed out of town by the two media buses, labelled "Into the Future" and "With Tony Blair". As their

occupants have noted, these three phrases have been cunningly crafted so that if the convoys gets out of order, the words will always fit together into a coherent message for the don't-knows and the disenchanted at the roadside.

One of the many things the Don't Knows don't know is Labour's policy on Europe. The Don't Knows don't listen to speeches or read policy documents. The Don't Knows don't pay attention to the political news on TV and in their papers. But, every five years, some of them do start tuning in to politics. They do switch on during the campaign.

Blair was keen to use his first day on the road to repeat his party's Euro referendum pledge because his polling suggested it had not registered with the public. He hoped the first day's campaigning would be covered in detail, allowing him to smuggle his increasingly Euro-sceptical attitude into the public consciousness. This was important because of the constant speculation that Major would move right on the single currency before polling day.

On the bus from Northampton to Derby, Alastair Campbell distributed the business speech Blair would be making at his second stop, drawing attention to the Euro passage: "We would not join in any fudged single currency or one not in Britain's interest - period." Inch by inch, Blair was distancing himself from the embrace of the Euro, so as not to be smothered by it either in the election or in government.

He delivered the speech at an event that was in itself a statement - a question-and-answer forum organised by the local Chamber of Commerce and CBI. This would not have been the traditional place to seek a Labour leader on his first campaigning day. But look where tradition has led most Labour leaders.

SO FAR, John Major had all the momentum of the Ancient Mariner. His campaign was becalmed. Sleaze continued to haunt the Tories like a punishment from fate, as if Major had shot an albatross along with all the other mistakes made after the 1992 election.

Labour smartly kept the sleaze story going by withdrawing its candidate in Tatton, Neil Hamilton's safe seat, and calling on the Liberal Democrats to do likewise so that a single anti-sleaze candidate could run against him. The LibDems agreed.

It seemed impossible for Major to get sleaze off the front pages. But at last, on the day of their manifesto launch, the Conservatives successfully trailed a pledge to allow non-working wives to transfer their tax allowances to their husbands. The newspapers bit. With an ICM poll showing Labour's lead down from 18 points to 14, the cuttings presented to Major on the morning of April 2 were like a puff of wind to the Ancient Mariner. (Incidentally, the job of preparing the daily cuttings for Major fell to a 25-year-old Tory official called George Osborne, who must have had one of the least rewarding jobs in politics).

The Tory manifesto was launched at a 10.30am press conference at Central Office. Several seats on the front row among the press had "reserved" signs for ministers. It was tempting to reflect that their seats in the Cabinet room were no longer reserved - even on ICM's figures, Labour would have a 130-seat majority.

Only the party chairman, Brian Mawhinney, and the deputy PM, Michael Heseltine, rated seats on the platform. Mawhinney called the questioners. Heseltine served no obvious purpose. It is hard to look enthusiastic when sitting silent like a dummy. Mawhinney looked like a funeral director. Major, standing at the lectern, did all the talking. He said Britain was booming.

> "Heseltine served no obvious purpose. It is hard to look enthusiastic when sitting silent like a dummy"

"This is the golden bequest the elected government will inherit," he said, trying not to sound frustrated at having to hand it over. The charts in the manifesto, though selective and slanted, nevertheless showed a growing economy with low inflation, falling unemployment and rising living standards. This combination was supposed to be a guarantee of political success. But the conventional rules of politics had broken down and the Conservatives could not understand why. They knew they had made mistakes, but thought that taking a penny off the basic rate in their last budget should have re-established them as tax-cutters. Bafflingly, it had not worked. Raising taxes in 1993-4 had been as fateful as the Ancient Mariner's ill-advised cruelty to birds. The Tories had killed stone dead the public's faith in them.

This went beyond tax. Labour had captured public opinion with its simple slogan: "You can't trust the Tories".

The more the Tories protested their success, the more arrogant and out of touch they sounded. The far-fetched claim that "Britain is Booming" fed the public perception of untrustworthiness - of ministerial pottiness - which in turn fuelled the feeling that it was time for a change.

"It is time for change," Major told the manifesto press conference. "Time for the next phase of Conservative prosperity".

Trying to present himself and his tired government as the men for a fresh start sounded even more eccentric than boasting of boom. Two sentences in his opening statement unwittingly highlighted Major's dilemma. He tried to reclaim the "One Nation" label from Blair, thus implicitly admitting that the Tories had drifted from the centre and needed dragging back. And he said of his economic success: "The importance of this isn't just that the country is doing well - it is what we can do with that success."

Both these statements made the case for Labour - that Britain needed a more caring government and could now afford to have one. This was precisely what people meant by time for change.

All this lay beneath the surface of Major's tortuous performance. More obvious was his problem with tax. He struggled embarrassingly with the tax question, fumbling his lines and even forgetting the reply he had - as TV cooks say - prepared earlier.

Tony Bevins of The Independent, who has the tact of a chainsaw, asked Major: "How on earth can you talk about lightening the tax burden when your own red book shows the tax burden has risen and will go on rising on your plans?" The red book is the tome put out by the Treasury every budget day. The latest had said the nation's tax burden had risen from just above 34 per cent when Labour lost office to just under 36 per cent and would go to 38 by 2002. The rising tax burden was Bevins' specialist subject. He was forever asking about it and the Tories had never yet been able to answer the question - why had the tax-cutting party allowed the overall tax burden to rise?

Major retreated into technicalities about tax "drift" - the tendency of more people to pay more tax as earnings rise. None of Major's advisors had yet found a way of selling tax drift to the public, or of explaining why the tax-cutting party could not find a way of offsetting it.

Later, John Sergeant of the BBC returned to the question of the Tory tax record. Suddenly, Major said he remembered what the answer should have been to the Bevins question and he was very sorry for not giving it at the time. The tax-raising tables in the red book showed that tax-cutting policies, like the ones he was now unveiling, were necessary.

This was one of the least convincing answers

any senior politician had ever given at such an important press conference. How could anyone pose as a tax-cutter while publishing tables in tablets of stone that said he was letting tax rise? It was an unanswerable question.

Labour was meanwhile briefing, back at the Commons, that Major's married couples' tax break would do nothing for five families in six. And it would cost upwards of £3 billion. Major insisted the cost was £1.2 billion. Anyone who looked at the published figures could see it was "eminently affordable".

But if the economic commentators were agreed on anything it was that the government spending plans published at budget time were implausibly tight. The new government, whoever formed it, would have to cut spending or raise taxes and probably put up interest rates too. So much for the golden bequest.

There now followed a deliciously bizarre scene. Labour called a 14.45 press conference to denounce the Tories for "spraying around" £15 billion worth of unfunded pledges - the married couples' wheeze, 20p income tax within five years, cutting inheritance and capital gains tax, etc.

"If Labour had made these promises without saying where the money would come from, you would never have heard the last of it," said Alastair Darling, the bright young Shadow Treasury Minister who was being pushed into the foreground of the campaign by his admirer, Tony Blair.

Gordon Brown, who had endured so much taunting from the Tories on where he was going to get his money from, tartly noted that the new Tory pledges were "not costed or funded".

We were now in the disorientating position of seeing the Tories make spending promises backed by vague talk of money generated by growth, while Labour had reduced its policies to the bare, affordable minimum.

THIS election is about trust," said Tony Blair. "For that very reason we make a virtue of the fact that our manifesto does not promise the earth."

Like John Major, he stood alone at a lectern, but he had his government-in-waiting on the stage with him at the Institute of Civil Engineers, across the road from the Treasury. Most of the still-shadow ministers sat in two rows, but four were given special prominence at a table beside the leader. The big four were John Prescott, Gordon Brown, Margaret Beckett and Robin Cook. It was an intriguing choice, especially Mrs Beckett, who had never been in the inner circle.

In government, the balance of power between these leading players would come to matter, but in Opposition only one player counted. The manifesto was very much Tony Blair's. He presented it as "neither a programme of the old left nor of the Conservatives". He spoke as if the leader of a new party, but he also stressed continuity, portraying himself as a leader taking Labour back to its true path.

"We are the broad-based movement for progress and justice our founders always dreamed of us becoming," he said. New Labour was "not a party of narrow class or sectional interests, but a true party of the people."

This was more than a neat phrase. The "people's party" used to be the conventional sneer against a party that was doomed by the disappearance of its working class support. Much had been written in the 1980s about the social inevitability of Labour's decline. Such talk would now be inconceivable.

Blairism had broken the stranglehold in which Thatcherism had taken British politics by appealing to the kind of aspiring people who had for a generation turned naturally to the Conservatives. John Major had never quite

"The election is not over until it's over. I don't think this is landslide country. As soon as you take the British people for granted, they remind you who is boss"

---

achieved his own -ism, but his election in 1992 had extended the life of the Thatcher coalition. Essex Man still voted alongside Eton old boys.

The significance of the 1997 election would be to break that coalition. Blairism had always been about more than winning an election, huge though that task was. It was about doing for the British left what Roosevelt had done in America, creating a lasting coalition that would make government by the party of the right an exception, rather than the rule.

The paradox of the manifesto of Blairism was that it set out to achieve this great aim by lowering expectations.

Blair's introduction said the manifesto contained a "limited" set of pledges. There was a very good reason for taking this minimalist approach. As he told the press conference: "I'm not standing here saying: vote for me on May 1 and on May 2 all you problems are solved. People have had enough of that."

This, to Blair, was the real gut issue of the campaign - that people had been taught by the Conservatives to have no faith in anything politicians told them. Important though detailed policy was, the key to victory was undetailed and very big - it was convincing people that you deserved their trust.

His phrase about May 1 and May 2 was a deliberate echo of Major's notorious pledge in 1992 that if you voted for him on Thursday, the economic recovery would begin on Friday. Blair's manifesto was a militant rejection of that kind of politics.

Blairism was about rigorously limiting your objectives to the ones that mattered and could be delivered. Blairism meant refusing to pretend that you could wave magic wands or produce instant solutions. It meant resisting the temptation to spend more than you could afford. Blairism meant saying no.

"This is the final nail in the coffin of the old

tax and spend agenda," he said. The manifesto section on the economy was headed: "We will promote personal prosperity for all." It dismissed as a myth the idea that extra spending was the solution to every problem. "New Labour is not about high taxes on ordinary families," it said.

"To encourage work and reward effort, we are pledged not to raise the basic or top rates of income tax throughout the next Parliament."

This statement would have been inconceivable even a few months before when the idea of a 50p rate at £100,000-a-year was being floated - though not by Tony Blair. The author of Blairism never had any doubt that his place in the history of the centre-left - and not just in Britain - was to find a way of delivering social justice without higher taxes. The legacy of the Thatcher-Reagan years was the impossibility of any party in a consumer democracy winning power while threatening higher personal taxation. The options for centre-left parties were to become neo-Conservatives or permanent Oppositions. Despite the cynical taunt that he was a closet Tory, Blair rejected both options. Blairism was socialism without taxes.

If you wanted to find work for 250,000 young unemployed, you did not raise a billion or two by raising the top rate of tax. What you did was find a different source of income.

"I have no time for the politics of envy," Blair said in his manifesto introduction.

He and Gordon Brown had found a source of income in the unpopular privatised utilities, whose excess profits would be tapped for a £3 billion programme of job creation.

Blairism meant that if you wanted to promise that every child would be taught in a class of fewer than 30 pupils, you did not take the money from the pay packets of the prosperous.

"I want a country in which people get on, do well, make a success of their lives," Blair wrote.

What you did was phase out the assisted places scheme, which subsidised a few thousand children's private schooling, and spent the money instead on all primary schools.

This was how Blairism achieved greater equality. This was Blairism re-distributing wealth and income. You didn't use the tax system, you gave the under-privileged and the ill-equipped the education and the training and the jobs that would enable them to get a fairer share of the nation's prosperity.

Blairism was about using the money saved

by the windfall tax job-creation programme to cut the country's benefit bills and re-invest the money saved in more education and training - not just for youngsters, but for single mothers who didn't want to be trapped on benefit and for older people who didn't want to be dumped from the jobs market in middle age.

Despite accusations of timidity, Blairism was about preventing the exploitation of the weak. The worst employers would have to pay the minimum wage and would have to recognise trade unions if a majority of their staff so voted in a secret ballot.

"The decent society and the prosperous economy go hand in hand," said Blair.

There was something else about Blairism. It meant admitting that your opponents were not all bad.

His introduction acknowledged: "Some things the Conservatives got right. We will not change them." Blairism meant treating the electorate like grown-ups. To forge his new coalition, he had to win the respect and the trust of people who had voted Tory and must therefore have believed at some stage that the Tories had got something right.

One reason for the low public tolerance of politicians was the playground mentality of con-ventional politics in which one side was all bad and the other all good. Blair rejected that.

None of which meant that Blairism was soft on its opponents. Blairism was only a month away from becoming real because the Conservatives had broken the trust of the people, and that was why Blair opened and finished his 45-minute press conference by saying the election was about trust.

Yes, the pledges mattered - the threat to close schools that failed their children, the offer of nursery places to all four-year-olds, the 2.5 per cent inflation target, retaining key elements of Tory trade union law, cutting NHS bureaucracy and using the money to shorten waiting lists, speedier punishment for young offenders, a new duty on councils to house the homeless, refusing to re-nationalise the railways now that privatisation was complete, giving devolution to Scotland and Wales, reforming the House of Lords, offering a referendum on the single currency.

Of course, that all mattered. But what mattered more was that, over the next month, the nation would look this young man in the eye and decide whether he could be trusted. If not, Blairism would vanish like a mirage. If the nation did put its faith in him, the Tories might be a long time repenting their sins in Opposition.

Tony Blair addresses the future at a school in the North East.

April 3
FOWL PLAY

THE untutored observer of the British constitution would have found it hard to explain how a man dressed as a chicken became the focal point of an election campaign. So would the tutored student, but here goes.

Long ago, Tony Blair had challenged John Major to a TV debate. Major was dismissive. It has always been the view that an incumbent does not agree to events that give his challenger the appearance of being his equal. But Conservative Central Office privately admitted all along that if Major was still far behind when the campaign arrived, then he would give the debate a go because by then Blair would be the man with most to lose.

And so Major agreed to a debate - or, rather, he presented it as his own idea, set out his terms and waited for the rival TV channels to fight for the right to screen it. This was a cunning manoeuvre. The competitive pressures on the TV companies ensured that Major got what he wanted - to avoid a three-way debate with both Blair and Paddy Ashdown and to avoid a "bearpit" in front of a live audience.

Blair was in a difficult position. He was angry with the broadcasters for falling in with Major's demands. And he did indeed have more to lose than the Prime Minister, who was by now in effect the challenger.

As negotiations dragged on, the Conservatives used the slow progress to suggest Blair was afraid of facing Major, who in their view would trounce the inexperienced Labour leader as he always did at Commons question time. This was not how question time actually felt to those who watched it twice a week from the gallery. Even when Major had the better of it, he usually did so by the kind of cheap point-scoring and loud abuse that pleased Tory backbenchers but would repel the public in a TV debate.

> Dr Mawhinney hired an actor to dress as a chicken and follow Mr Blair around. Those who suspected that Dr Mawhinney had no sense of humour were clearly wrong

Nevertheless, Brian Mawhinney pushed his line. He had had few successes so far and was determined to make best use of the debate-about-the-debate. Finally, when the talks reached deadlock, Dr. Mawhinney declared: "Mr. Blair is chicken."

He said it with the satisfied air of a man who had got the outcome he wanted.

Seeking to elevate the intellectual tone of the campaign, Dr Mawhinney hired an out-of-work actor to dress as a chicken and follow Mr. Blair around. Those who suspected that Dr Mawhinney had no sense of humour were clearly wrong.

Mawhinney's chicken made its debut on the day of Labour's manifesto launch. Pre-emptively, the Mirror dressed a reporter as a headless chicken and sent him round to Central Office. Alex Aitken from the press office was needlessly sent out to turn the headless chicken away. Special Branch would never have allowed a potential assassin in a fluffy yellow suit to get near the Prime Minister. Anyway, the bird had no credentials and would not even have made it past Central Office security. All Mr Aitken achieved was a scuffle which made first-rate pictures for the Mirror.

Meanwhile word had spread through the animal kingdom. Two bears turned up at the Labour manifesto launch. They were not from Tory HQ or the Mirror. When asked where they came from, they replied: "The woods". They explained that their purpose was to protest that the election was becoming a circus.

As well as the headless chicken, the Mirror despatched a fox to frighten the Tory fowl away.

At Blair's next stop - walking about in Bayswater - he was attended by a rhinoceros. When asked where he was from, the rhino replied: "South Africa." He was less precise about his purpose, having come without a soundbite as neat as the bears'. The travelling

press, for whom this was much better fun than analysing the manifesto, questioned the rhino closely without getting any clear answers. Unkind souls suggested this was always going to be the case on the Blair tour. Being precise animals, journalists dislike the unexplained. The rhino left them puzzled. Getting back on the bus, they were heard discussing his purpose apparently in all seriousness: "But what point was the rhino making?"

Blair was heading for Scotland. So was the chicken, by plane - chickens cannot fly that far unaided. What would Tory donors think of this use of their cash - how would Asil Nadir like his hard-earned money being squandered on flying an actor in fancy dress to Edinburgh?

The waste said little for Tory economics. The more frugal Mirror despatched a second fox from its Glasgow lair. It caught up with the Tory chicken in Stirling, where Blair was gladhanding shoppers. The day's second scuffle ensued. Thanks to the intrepid Mirror fox, the chicken never got near the Labour leader.

Before leaving town, Blair generously invited the tired, much-travelled chicken to dinner, with the pledge that he would not be on the menu. The chicken declined, perhaps fearing that this might be Labour's first broken promise.

Next day, the chicken entered the Tory leadership odds at 500-1.

Put in there: New Labour interacts with the new generation.

April 4
TROUBLE IN SCOTLAND

THE newspaper reviews of Tony Blair's manifesto performance would have gone up in lights had he been a West End musical. But what plays well in London does not always play well in the country. The following morning, he was mauled by his Scottish critics.

He had ensured himself an unhappy visit with some remarks in an interview on the plane from Stansted to Edinburgh. Inevitably, the problem was caused by the West Lothian question - how can you justify allowing Scottish MPs at Westminster to vote on English matters once you have devolved some of Westminster's power to a Scottish parliament? The question had first been asked by the Labour backbencher Tam Dalyell when he was MP for West Lothian. Like all theological questions, it had no answer. You simply had to have faith that devolution was right.

The Scotsman's political editor, John Penman, put his version of the fabled query by asking whether Blair's Sedgefield constituents thought it unfair that Scottish MPs would still be able to vote on English matters.

Blair said he would tell his English constituents that "as far as we are concerned sovereignty rests with me as an English MP and that's the way it will stay."

Penman then moved to the other difficult question raised by Labour's devolution policy - would he, as British Prime Minister, ever try to over-rule the Scottish Parliament if it used its most contentious power, to increase income tax? Trying to explain that authorities do not necessarily use their constitutional powers, Blair said the Scottish Parliament's powers would be "like those of any local authority". It was, he added, "like any parish council". What he meant was that local authorities, from parish councils up,

Put simply, he was not prepared to utter the words 'tax' and 'up' in the same sentence however rhetorical because he knew his words would be used against him.

---

had the right to raise revenue, but didn't always use it.

The analogy was constitutionally sound, but politically insensitive. It sounded as though he were belittling the proposed Scottish Parliament as no grander than an English parish council. His assertion that ultimate sovereignty would remain at Westminster was again constitutionally sound - in a United Kingdom, that must technically be the case. But it sounded as though England would reserve the right to over-rule the Scots. This impression was deepened by his constitutionally-dubious claim that Westminster sovereignty rested "with me as an English MP", rather than with Parliament.

All this Englishness was not calculated to guarantee a warm welcome in Scotland. Alex Salmond, leader of the Scottish Nationalists, said there was "a touch of megalomania" about Blair's personal attitude to sovereignty. And the parish council quote was such a gift that he would be posting it through every door in Scotland. Salmond was exaggerating when he said Blair's interview had blown the contest wide open in Scotland, but it had guaranteed a rough reception from the press.

The launch of Labour's Scottish manifesto was dominated by hostile questions on devolution, to such an extent that Blair eventually pleaded: "Is there anybody who would like to ask a question about anything else?"

Blair had never got on with the Scottish media. The contrast between his reception in Glasgow and London was stark. The hounds of the Scottish media were less easily faced down than their English counterparts. One of them accused Blair of getting in a muddle whenever he came to Scotland. Before long the press conference was going round in tight circles on the same question - would you over-rule the Scottish parliament if it tried to raise tax?

Clearly he would not. By definition, if you cede a tax-raising power to a devolved parliament, that means you do not over-rule it - otherwise you haven't ceded the power at all. But Blair was reluctant to spell out the obvious. The reason was that if he ever admitted even the remotest possibility of tax being raised by the new parliament, the Tories would use it to label him an instinctive tax-raiser.

Put simply, he was not prepared to utter the words "tax" and "up" in the same sentence, however theoretical, because he knew his words would be twisted and used against him.

So, over and over, he repeated that Labour's policy was not to raise tax in the new Scottish Parliament, any more than it was at Westminster. Over and over, the Scottish media demanded to know if that meant London might over-rule Edinburgh.

The two sides became equally exasperated. Blair kept smiling, but his irritation was clearer and clearer as he spelled out his answer more and more painstakingly. He sounded like a schoolmaster who cannot understand why a dim class fails to grasp the theory of relativity. The usual courtesies broke down as journalists stopped waiting to be called and shouted questions over each other.

It was such a bad press conference that it was reported nationally as Blair's first stumble of the campaign. Although the launch of the Liberal Democrat manifesto led the evening news, with its pledge of a penny on tax to be spent on education, the second story showed an uncomfortable Blair fending off hostile questions. Major was slick enough to re-write that night's speech to accuse Blair of muddle. Major had scented blood.

Below: Tony Blair's conviction shines out as he addresses a city centre crowd from the battlebus platform.

April 4
UNTROUBLED
IN MIDDLE
ENGLAND

IT IS odd that Blair tended to have a harder time in Scotland, Labour's kingdom, than in the English marginals where Labour had struggled so long.

From Glasgow he flew to Manchester Airport and went by bus to Kidsgrove in the Tory-held Staffordshire Moorlands seat, for a question-and-answer session with voters. Labour had advertised the meeting in the local paper, hoping to attract "real people", rather than committed supporters. Leaflets had been sent to voters identified by canvassers as disillusioned Tories who were not sure about Labour.

The meeting was held at the Victoria Hall, a little joke to emphasise the contrast with John Major's rally for Tory members that night at the Albert Hall. Blair wanted to make the point that he was reaching out to the people who would decide the election, while Major was apparently shoring up his core vote.

As Blair said in his opening remarks: "They are preaching to the converted. I am here persuading people who are not yet converted."

It is always hard to tell if audiences of so-called real voters are in fact the real thing. There must have been many Labour members who snapped up tickets on the hotline number advertised in the Stoke Sentinel. They presumably were the ones who cheered the Labour theme "Things Can Only Get Better" just before Blair's entrance. The hour's questioning was not hostile, unlike the Scottish media's. But then, even ex-Tories in the audience must have been leaning strongly

It is one thing to tell well-paid journalists that you are not going to spend money on eye tests, dentistry, schools, higher education ... quite another to do it to the voters

towards Blair before taking the trouble to turn up. One man asked about the danger of union power under Labour, but most of the questions were anxious inquiries from people who clearly did not believe Britain was booming. Most of them wanted more money spent on whatever their own chief concern was. If there was any suspicion of Blair, it seemed to be that he wasn't throwing enough money at the country's problems.

It is one thing to tell well-paid journalists that you are not going to spend money on eye tests, dentistry, schools, higher education – quite another to do it to the voters. Blair did so, to every one.

When a man shook his head in disappointment over student loans, Blair said: "This is the core of what I believe in. I'm not going to spin you what is a lie - that we can put everything right through the tax system. Because we can't."

He got his biggest cheer when he said: "Don't let the Tories frighten you about Labour. You should be a darned sight more frightened if the Tories got back for another term than if Labour wins".

Either Labour had done a brilliant job of packing the audience, or this slice of Middle England was jammed full of ex-Tories in no mood to return to Major.

On the stairs going out, two middle-aged ladies said they were lifelong Tory voters who were switching to Labour. "We're impressed," they kept saying. Why? "He's honest," said one. "He didn't make rash promises like other politicians," said the other.

April 5
AT HOME

T IS just gone 10.00 on a Saturday morning and Trimdon Labour Club is packed. Members outnumber the media, but only just. This is Tony Blair's political home and he's due any minute for his adoption meeting.

It is 14 years since Tony Blair first travelled hopefully to Trimdon, a village in the countryside north of Durham. It was here that he had his first great slice of luck. When he first came to Trimdon, the 1983 general election was already under way and the young Blair had yet to find a seat. When he heard there was a late vacancy in a new seat near Durham, where he had spent much of his youth, he drove north.

First, Blair had to find someone to back him. Trimdon ward had not yet made a nomination. Blair had some trouble finding the home of the

> "We had this young man, intelligent, charming, with all these ideas about changing the party. The thing is he did it. It started here. All those changes started here."

branch secretary, John Burton. When he did, he almost didn't go in, sitting in the car asking himself - what am I doing here? Burton and a few friends were watching football. One of them, Terry Ward, takes up the story. "It was his last chance saloon," he says. "We were watching the European Cup Winners' Cup Final and he had to wait until the match was over before we would talk to him."

The young stranger talked them into nominating him.

"He was bright as a button and you could tell he was his own man," says Ward, though he was not so convinced as the others. These were still the days when a moderate like Blair was a rarity in a Labour movement veering left in Opposition.

Ward, like many who were to

Below: Tony Blair gets some words of encouragement from his father Leo.

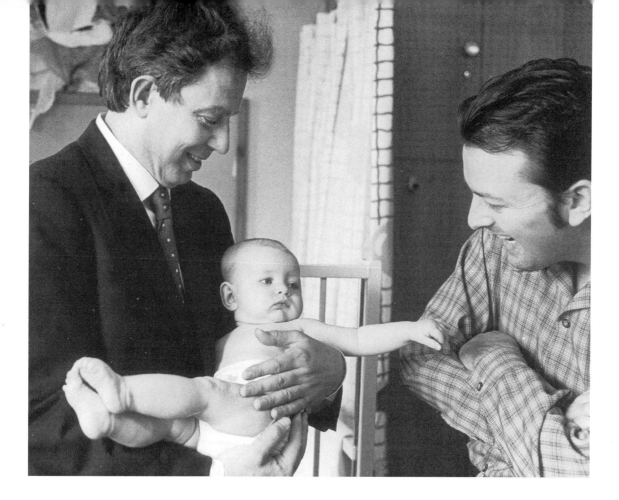

Little Rebecca Kelly finds herself being held by Tony Blair in a South Cleveland hospital

follow, has long become convinced that Blair's New Labour strategy is what the party needed.

Standing among the jostling crowd at the Labour Club waiting for the Labour leader to arrive, he says: "This is absolutely great. This is history. Trimdon village is never going to be the same. I know he likes to be cautious, but we know he's going to be Prime Minister. Even in that short time of talking to him that first night, there was something special there. He's never any different, you know. When he disagrees with you, he tells you."

Among Blair's home crowd, there are journalists not only from London, but from Germany, France, Switzerland and America, though Joe Klein of the New Yorker, author of the bestselling campaign novel Primary Colours, is the only foreign journalist given the privilege of accreditation to Blair's bus. At Trimdon, Klein is going to be allowed to follow Blair into the small bar, which has little room for the world's media, to watch the future Prime Minister mixing with Englishmen drinking pints of beer. But first Blair has to be formally adopted as Labour candidate.

There's a cheer as Blair at last comes in with John Burton, the man who did more than anyone to get the young stranger a start in politics back in 1983. When Blair failed to make the original

shortlist, it was Burton who talked the general management committee into adding a seventh name so that Blair could convince the constituency party to adopt him. This time, 1997, Sedgefield will not need convincing.

"Delegates and members," says Burton, now Blair's agent and constituency chairman. "I know I have a reputation for crying..." He recalls Blair's unexpected arrival in Trimdon.

"We had this young man - intelligent, charismatic - with all these ideas about changing the party, about bringing it up to date. The thing is ... he did it. It started here. All those changes started here.

"It is a great honour to introduce him for his adoption speech. We have already printed the Tony Blair posters, mind you."

"You know I don't like anything being taken for granted," says Blair.

This is an emotional moment. Politics is a hard, cynical game, but it is played by real people, especially out in the constituencies where the unrewarding work is done by thousands of people like Burton and friends. They mean a lot to Blair. When people say he is a closet Conservative who has destroyed the heart and soul of the Labour movement, they should remind themselves that he could have done nothing without the support of these people in Trimdon. It was their longing for a reformed,

sensible Labour Party that convinced him he was right to launch and maintain his revolution.

"This is where everything all began for me politically and where I have learned so much," Blair tells his people.

"I hope I have given something to this constituency party, but I have learned a lot here. I have seen decent people crying out for a different kind of Labour Party, that could rise above the problems of the past.

"I remember that 1983 election. John stopped me watching the news because it made me so depressed.

"All the way through you kept faith in me. It was difficult because we were turning things over that people thought were cherished.

"You supported me all the way through and without you I could never have become leader of the Labour Party. It could never have happened because all the way through I had the foundation of my career solid here in Sedgefield. When I became leader I knew there was a place I could always come back to for some decent common

sense. "I remember all those years ago how we seem to have lost our way and now we have found it.

Tony Blair relaxes among friends at Trimdon Labour Club

"One other little word to John. He is the person whose house I very nearly failed to find in Trimdon all those years ago. He is one of the best political mentors anyone could have.

"The media always write about all these people I am supposed to be consulting. I get more sense out of John than I do out of most politicians in the big bad world of Westminster.

"We never forget that our real aim is not changing the Labour Party but changing the country. That great journey began here. I hope on May 1st I can come back here and say that journey has resulted in an election victory."

John Burton then does the formalities. "I know he will change the country. I know that. So will someone please move his adoption as our MP."

Tony Blair is the only nominee.

MUDDLED. Inexperienced. Untrustworthy. The conservatives made brilliantly cynical use of Tony Blair's first campaign wobble. Building rapidly on the foundations of his bad Friday in Glasgow, they claimed by Sunday morning to have identified three Blair U-turns and by Monday morning five.

It scarcely mattered what they were, nor how flimsy the evidence of Blair's swift collapse. What mattered was the use of the same words over and over on TV and radio. Muddled. Inexperienced. Untrustworthy.

Indeed, it suited the Tories that the issues involved were so obscure and the mistakes allegedly made were so negligible. That lessened the risk of detail getting in the way of the message. All that came through to a semi-interested public was the repeated mantra. Muddled. Inexperienced. Untrustworthy.

No doubt the first proper week of campaigning had ended less than perfectly for Labour, but the claim that Blair was collapsing was as exaggerated as the Conservatives' claims for the economy.

Major, interviewed on the BBC's Breakfast With Frost, said: "They have had three years to prepare their manifesto and in three days it's falling apart."

His evidence was that Blair had already reneged on his promise of a tax-raising parliament for Scotland, had welched on his promises to the unions and had embraced privatisation. During the day, U-turns on terrorism and the single currency were added to the list of muddled untrustworthiness.

Left: A thoughtful moment as the pressure mounts.

Most of this was very silly. On Scotland, Labour had simply confirmed its commitment to a par-

To go as far as to call him a scoundrel was not credible. People did not think that of Tony Blair, though they thought it of some Tories.

liament with decision-making powers on tax, but said the party would not itself raise tax in Scotland. Was Mr. Blair supposed to say he would keep tax down in England while stinging the Scots?

On trade unions, TUC leaders had asked him to give part-time workers the same rights as full-timers. Blair had ruled that out some time ago and his reply was that he would indeed not concede this right. It was a funny kind of U-turn. The U-turn would have been to have bowed to the last-minute union demands. On the single currency, Robin Cook's Sunday statement that Britain would probably not join during the next parliament was part of the same distancing process that the Tory party had gone through. Either both parties were U-turning, or neither; or perhaps both were being sensibly cautious.

Terrorism should never have been dragged into the political mudwrestling. It was a grotesque abuse by Michael Howard to score points off Labour's objections to some aspects of the Prevention of Terrorism Act in the wake of the bomb scare that postponed the Grand National. Shadow Home Secretary Jack Straw responded that an incoming Labour government would operate the Act on taking office. But whatever the merits of the argument, the bigger question was whether any politician had the right to start a dispute over terrorism in the shadow of an IRA outrage. Mr. Howard had himself proposed and secured a pre-election agreement with Mr. Straw that nothing like this would be done during the campaign, because it could only help the terrorists. In practice, this agreement clearly did not prevent the Home Secretary stooping as low as he pleased in search of rightwing support.

The one legitimate charge of muddle was against Blair's new line on privatisation. His office let it be known to the Sunday papers that his Monday speech on the economy would announce a review of government services, land and buildings to see if any assets could be sold.

One source, referring back to the battle to drop the Clause Four commitment to nationalisation, called Mr. Blair's impending announcement as "the final piece in the jigsaw".

The only trouble with this argument was that at the manifesto launch Blair had brushed aside a question from Peter Riddell of The Times about the problem of filling the "black hole" in government spending plans if Labour halted current privatisations and denied itself the receipts.

These were estimated at £1.5 billion and a party that had made a virtue of carefully costing its commitments could hardly ignore the loss of such a sum. Why had Blair acted as if there was no problem on Thursday, only to make a landmark statement on the issue on Monday? It seemed that his determination to keep the initiative by making regular agenda-setting statements had for once backfired. Keeping such an important announcement back for a few days thrust him into the Tory trap. Because this important change was made post-manifesto, it looked as though Labour was being pushed into policymaking on the hoof.

Worse still, as recently as the Labour conference six months earlier, Transport spokesman Andrew Smith had promised to fight one of the proposed privatisations, of air traffic control. An impassioned clip of Andrew Smith's conference speech was shown repeatedly to Labour's embarrassment on the TV news.

The Conservatives had a point. It did look a bit odd for Labour to have woken up to the problem of the £1.5 billion privatisation gap this late. Though Blair's plea for an end to dogmatic divisions between public and private ownership sounded refreshing on the TV bulletins, the shift seemed a last-minute decision made under pressure. It invited the Tories to ask what else Blair might change. The chance to turn the word "trust" against him was irresistible.

As usual, the Tories overdid it. Ken Clarke called Labour leaders "unprincipled scoundrels". This surely was not in tune with the public mood. Voters might be susceptible to the argument that Blair was a little too ready to say what they wanted to hear - polls suggested this was a potential weakness, as it was bound to be for a leader who had had to change so much to make his party electable. But to go so far as to call him a scoundrel was not credible. People did not think that of Tony Blair, though they thought it of some Tories.

The whole problem came down to whether the public was likely to give Blair the benefit of the doubt in the face of these Tory charges. When a man makes changes, he can equally be described as a brave reformer or a weakling in retreat, depending on taste. There was surely no question that the public saw Blair's changes to Labour as strength rather than weakness. This was the difficulty the new Tory line had. The picture of Tony Blair panicking into muddled changes conflicted with the image he had risked so much to establish, particularly during the Clause Four campaign.

Nevertheless, this spirited Tory onslaught was Blair's first serious examination under fire and the first real test of the public's attitude towards him. The Conservatives were quite right to give it a go and their sharp performance over the weekend of April 5-6 showed, if nothing else, that they could still bite.

April 7
WHITE KNIGHT

THE man in the white suit strode into the election campaign on a quiet Monday afternoon when the parties seemed to have run out of their initial puff. It was a slow news day and there was nothing better to do than stroll across Parliament Square to the Institute of Civil Engineers to watch Martin Bell announce his campaign as the anti-sleaze candidate for Tatton, Neil Hamilton's ultra-safe seat.

He came in by himself, sat fiddling nervously with his watch and said that if anyone wanted to talk privately "come and see me afterwards". The man in the white suit didn't even have a spin doctor.

What he did have was a spotless reputation. During the Bosnian war, Martin Bell and his trademark "lucky white suit" had nagged at the national conscience. He had established himself as a man who cared about a tragedy that most of us preferred to ignore and we admired him for not turning away. One BBC colleague unkindly called him a "quasi Mother Teresa figure", but it caught the public feeling for a figure whose appearance of selfless integrity made him the very opposite of the man he was taking on. Nobody would ever offer Martin Bell a free holiday at the Paris Ritz or an envelope stuffed with £50 notes.

It was inevitably Tony Bevins who asked Bell if he had any skeletons. "I have been searching my cupboard and I find it at the moment pretty bare."

Bell said he had never had an expenses return queried in 30 years at the BBC, except when an illiterate New Delhi taxi driver had been unable to write him a receipt.

Would he accept a campaign gift from Mohammed Al-Fayed, the millionaire alleged to have proffered used notes and the freedom of the Ritz? Bell said he would accept £100 at most "as long as it was not in a brown envelope".

He was caught out when asked who had hired the room for his press conference. He didn't know.

He came in by himself, sat fiddling nervously with his watch and said that if anyone wanted to talk privately they could "come and see me afterwards."

"I probably should know". Andrew Pierce of The Times told him the Labour Party had paid £375.

"I am perfectly willing to pay here and now," said Bell and when the press conference ended he asked Pierce for the address to send his money to.

It would be 24 hours before Tatton Conservatives met to decide whether they dared put up Hamilton against the man in the white suit. Meanwhile sleaze was back at the top of the news. The words "muddled", "inexperienced" and "untrustworthy" had slipped off the agenda.

Bell travelled north and called his first local press conference the following morning, on Knutsford Heath. It was reduced to farce by the appearance of Neil Hamilton and, more important, his wife Christine. Thanks to the silence Hamilton had so far maintained, Mrs Hamilton had become his spokeswoman and turned herself into landmark on the election landscape. The Daily Mail's Lynda Lee Potter wrote a paean to Mrs. Hamilton on the theme: "If Britain had more women like this, we would still have an empire."

Martin Bell can have faced few sterner tests of his courage than Mrs Hamilton on Knutsford Heath.

"Do you accept that my husband is innocent until proven guilty?" she kept asking. Bell said he did. This was not a woman to disagree with. She was a sort of poor man's Margaret Thatcher - except that, if the allegations were all true, her silent husband was hardly a poor man. Now he too spoke up, inquiring unforbiddingly if Bell did indeed accept he was innocent until proven guilty. Softened up by Mrs H, Martin Bell agreed.

This episode, played out in a tight media huddle, made marvellous television. It may have done something to save Mrs Hamilton's husband from losing his nomination. That evening, Tatton Tories confirmed that Christine Hamilton would have a candidate for a husband. They voted on a show of hands to back him.

THE real world was finding it hard to force its way into the election. Now, twice within 24 hours, it made valiant attempts. First, the churches produced a conscience-tugging report on unemployment. Then, the Institute for Fiscal Studies came out with a heavyweight analysis of the parties' economic policies.

Between them, these two reports formed a users' guide to the state of the country and did much to explain the apparent conundrum of impending government defeat during a boom.

The Churches of Britain and Ireland inquiry team - gathered together by the Bishop of Liverpool, the Rt Rev David Sheppard - had been "shocked and saddened" by what they saw. Everywhere, riches and poverty were increasing side by side .The report cast doubt on the accuracy of the unemployment figures and criticised the big parties for focusing on tax cuts for the "favoured majority".

Their description of Major's Britain jarred with the happy language coming from ministers, led by the man who had once said he wanted a country at ease with itself. It explained why the nation refused to show its gratitude to the government.

The real-world picture was reinforced by the IFS, which said the government's tax rises had cost the average family £7 a week. Labour said this vindicated its charge that the Tories had broken their 1992 tax promises. The Tories pointed out that the IFS also said rising living standards had made the same family more than £700 better off, vindicating their claim to have delivered greater prosperity.

The two statements were not as contradictory

> "If I stood for election on this platform and made the promises they made, I would not have the gall to ask the people to trust me again."

as they looked. In a growing economy, incomes rise. It was up to the government to convince the voters that ministers deserved the credit. It was failing. The people seemed to feel they had earned that extra £700 by their own efforts, not the government's.

What was the government's responsibility was how much it took in tax. The take had gone up, however you measured it, in pounds and pence or by percentage of national output. The Conservatives were trying their best to persuade voters otherwise. They seemed to be failing. Yes, people were better off . But, yes, the alleged party of low tax was levying higher taxes.

Wednesday, 9 April, was the fifth anniversary of John Major's 1992 victory. Labour's inevitable theme for the day was the broken manifesto promises on tax.

Tony Blair stood dramatically at his lectern in the press conference room at Millbank Tower and held up the '92 Tory Manifesto.

He said: "If I had stood for election on this platform and made the promises they made, I would not have the gall to ask the British people to trust me again. Yet this is what the Conservatives do today."

He contrasted his own platform - "promises all the way through that can be kept".

One of the jargon phrases of modern campaigning is "on message". Both sides try to set themselves a message for the day and keep to it, while each tries to push the other "off message". This was a day when the Conservatives were more intent than usual on pushing Labour off message. There was no getting round the broken promises, no defending the '92 manifesto. Distractions must be found. Michael Heseltine

Previous pages: Getting the message across to the ever-present media circus

volunteered himself as distractor-in-chief.

His first attempt was an extraordinary claim: "Tony Blair is cracking under the strain." This was not completely out of the blue. Central Office had tried to talk some of the Sunday papers into writing that Blair had been sweating profusely at his manifesto launch, like a man under strain, and wearing an earpiece to allow his manipulators to prompt him. Many man-hours were wasted by picture editors searching for evidence. None was found. This bizarre attempted smear said much about the Tories' failure to understand what they were up against. Some of them really believed Blair was such a hollow man that he needed his head filled with live commentary on the best line to take from Alastair Campbell, presumably with Peter Mandelson piped simultaneously into the other ear. It was little wonder that the Conservatives found it so hard to take on Tony Blair while deluding themselves into thinking there was nothing to him. Under-estimating an opponent is usually fatal.

Heseltine himself was not that stupid. His "crack-up" comment was straight from the Heseltine book of campaigning, which lays down that nobody ever got anywhere by under-stating his case. He didn't believe Blair was having a breakdown. He did believe the Labour leader was a little shaky on a policy or two and it was worth trying to needle him into mistakes. Once your opponents start making mistakes, there's no knowing what openings might offer themselves to an opportunist.

The attempt to nettle Blair was a failure. The first chance the TV crews had to get Blair's reaction was at the end of a boat trip in Bristol. Cherie was there, very fetching in a sailor's top. Blair had taken his jacket off - carrying it was one of Alastair's many responsibilities. Tony and Cherie were at their most easygoing, smiling in the sun.

Mr. Blair, are you cracking up? "As you can see, I'm in very good shape," he said. He called the Tories "desperate people".

Blair's morning press conference - holding up the "manifesto of broken promises" played well on the lunchtime news. But Heseltine wasn't finished yet.

John Prescott gave an interview for ITN's 12.30 bulletin which was shown while the Blair boat was docking. By the time the Blair buses drove out of Bristol for Exeter, Heseltine was on

the BBC's World At One putting a Tory spin on the Prescott comments as only Heseltine could. Prescott had "spat in the eye of his leader". There was "open warfare" in the Labour Party.

What Prescott had actually said was: "We don't have a policy of directly wanting to privatise anything, quite frankly. But we will face the realities of what has to be done with public assets." He added that Labour was "quite prepared in some cases, perhaps, to consider selling" some public assets.

While there might be some debate about slight differences in tone, this was hardly war. But that was not the point. The Tories had to keep on needling not only Blair, but his senior colleagues, in the hope that someone might eventually over-react.

Relaxed, bathed in sunshine, very much "on message", Blair stopped with his people's platform in the most lovely setting at the Cathedral Close, Exeter: "They were re-elected on a manifesto every single part of which they then broke," he said.

Back on the buses, Blair and his attendant media headed for Plymouth, arriving at the Moat House, behind the Hoe, in brilliant weather. We were promised "an evening's entertainment" at the Guildhall. This sounded suspiciously Sheffield Rally-like. But the atmosphere was not so much presidential as provincial theatre, with a saxophone group and some engagingly-obvious jokes from a political comedy trio. Roy Marsden, TV's Commander Adam Dalgleish, compered. The warm-up for Blair was Patrick Stewart, from Star Trek.

Stewart's speech lifted proceedings above the provincial. As one of the travelling US correspondents said: "Never mind Blair - this guy really is famous."

Stewart, with his deep voice and genuine star presence, gave a stirring speech on the meaning of Blair. He quoted the widow in Arthur Miller's Death Of A Salesman, talking about the plight of ordinary people: "Attention must be paid."

He said: "I am here tonight because I think New Labour is the party that will pay attention, will listen to the weakest voices, will stand up for those who can't stand up for themselves. I am convinced that a Labour government led by Tony Blair will pay attention."

AND then the polls turned. Or, rather, a poll turned. The news reached Blair as he left Plymouth in the dusk. MORI in The Times had Labour down six, the Tories up six. True, the lead was still a historically huge 15, but this was the first hint of a sign of the comeback that everyone had expected for most of the last three years. It would not matter unless other polls followed and, indeed, the same day's Gallup in the Telegraph had Labour's lead up one. But what Labour didn't want was for this potential setback to coincide with a policy problem. Unfortunately it did.

The questioning at Blair's Millbank press conference next morning ranged widely - nobody was yet taking the narrowing lead too seriously, but there was a definite feeling in the room that this was a time to probe for weakness. Blair was questioned about tax, competitive tendering, the possibility of riots if he implemented his zero-tolerance crime policy. Blair was happy to take all comers. He even called Peter Hitchens of The Express, a one-man awkward squad who had listed in that morning's paper the questions he said Labour wouldn't let him ask.

Handed a roving microphone, Hitchens chose from his list the one about the Blairs' choice of school. How could Blair say he wanted the same for every child as for his own when he had sent his son to the London Oratory?

The choice of the Oratory had caused Blair more trouble in the party than anything in his leadership, including the scrapping of Clause Four. It was a grant-maintained Catholic school which was reputed to use its interviews on the family's religious status as a cloak for covert selection.

Blair pointed out that if he won the election he would be the first Prime Minister with children in the state system.

"That's not a proper answer," snapped

> Harold Macmillan said that the worst problem for a Prime Minister was "events, dear boy, events."
> In other words, the unexpected and the unplanned.

Hitchens. Blair tried to call another question, but Hitchens persisted. "Peter, will you please sit down..."

"...no answer..."

"Peter, please tried to contain yourself".

Hitchens did get on the bulletins, but he had failed to ask the agenda-setting question. That came from the unaggressive Robin Oakley, Political Editor of the BBC.

Oakley wanted to come back to the privatisation problem. He had a fax from the air traffic controllers' union to their members saying they had been assured as late as mid March by Labour's Transport team that they were opposed to air traffic privatisation - so just when had the policy changed? This was a difficult question because Labour's main defence against the U-turn charge was that Margaret Beckett had said air traffic privatisation was under review on February 23. So how come the transport team had been telling the unions in March that privatisation was off? This question followed Blair across the country.

The travelling press had to set off before the leader, while he did the Jimmy Young Programme on Radio Two. After some difficulty tuning in, the bus radio played the live interview to a group that was already becoming dangerously bored with the leader's usual script, by now utterly familiar. Some started joining in with the better-known answers. But they were silent when JY tucked into privatisation. This was off script, off message. It was a whiff of danger. The bus was on full "story alert" - the chance of the candidate saying something that unravelled on him.

JY has an unfair reputation as a soft interviewer. Because he is polite, it is impossible to be rude to him. This gives him an advantage over the supposedly tougher interviewers. The interviewee has to remain as courteous and helpful as JY seems to be, when it might suit them to have a go back at a bullying host.

Tony Blair prepares for yet another on-the-road TV interview.

Wasn't this union fax odd? asked Jimmy.

Blair said he didn't believe the union official involved had actually spoken to a member of the shadow ministerial team. Anyway, Margaret had already said the position was under review.

But who did the union speak to, then?

"I'm not sure," said Blair. "I simply don't know. We have made inquiries."

He could be sure the papers would too. By now well up the M40, the travelling press rang their offices. They had a story. This was just the kind of whodunnit that brings politics to life. Here was another Labour policy found clubbed to death - who did it and when?

Millbank Tower was on full alert too. Mandelson's campaign HQ had set up a system by which every member of the Shadow Cabinet could be bleeped simultaneously, to ensure that nobody strayed off message. Bleepers now went off all over the country. The line was: "If elected, we will face hard choices ... we cannot rule out looking at the government plans we will inherit on air traffic control."

By the time the bus reached Redditch and Blair had caught up by helicopter, the story was leading the BBC news and damage control was under way. The union was now saying it had in fact been told the policy was under review. Andrew Smith was fielded on the World At One. He said the relevant conversation had not been with a shadow minister, but a researcher.

As the media gathered in a school hall to hear Blair address sixth formers, his staff passed a press release over the heads of the children to reporters, seeking to clarify the position. It insisted the union had been told the policy was under review.

It was much ado about very little, when measured by public interest in the issue involved. The election was hardly going to turn on the future of the air traffic control system. But it was a rare case of Labour being shoved "off message", another test of the Blair team's ability to deal with the unexpected and the unplanned. That it was so unfamiliar was a tribute to Blair's dazzling performance in dictating the political agenda for three years, with barely a slip. But Harold Macmillan once said that the worst problem for a Prime Minister was "events, dear boy, events" - in other words, the unexpected and the unplanned. The air traffic controversy was a foretaste of life in government for a team that was used to creating events, not coping with them on the run. The real test of a politician is events beyond his control.

Blair was, to his credit, paying the price for honesty. He could have spent the campaign batting away the problem of how to replace the privatisation receipts that would be lost by scrapping the sell-offs. It would be easy enough to find a form of words to cover it - look at the books when in power, and so forth. But Blair

was determined to confront such problems openly, believing honesty would have its reward. Honesty sometimes brought punishment too, though. He had opened up a series of consequential questions that inevitably followed on from his boldness in facing the full implications of inheriting Tory spending plans.

The appearance of Labour disarray was the flip side of another Blair strength. A leader who knows where he is going sometimes arrives well ahead of his party and it did look as though the air traffic controversy was a revealing case of Labour scrambling to catch up with its leader in some semblance of order.

EUROPE was still out there, the lurking issue, somewhere beneath the gently rippling surface of an election campaign that was still awaiting its first real storm. Finally the killer issue surged up from the deep, in the unlikely shape of Angela Browning, the parliamentary under-secretary for agriculture. Mrs. Browning, a hitherto blamelessly dull junior minister, wrote in her local election newsletter in Tiverton that she feared the single currency would mean "the end of sovereignty of the nation state and if that is what is offered I have made it very clear I will not support it".

It had long been feared that scores, maybe hundreds, of Conservative candidates would break with the cautious official "wait and see" policy on the Euro and issue true blue personal manifestos.

Perhaps it would be more accurate to say it had long been hoped that this would occur. The response of the Tory high command to the Tiverton Declaration was interesting. There was a complete absence of panic, not a hint of recrimination. The usual outbreak of Tory bloodletting over Europe did not happen. There was no storm. Major calmly said there was no question of sacking Angela Browning and Welsh Secretary William Hague was put up on the lunchtime news to say there would be no sanctions against anyone over their election addresses.

This was a curious re-definition of collective responsibility. Ministers were being granted the freedom to declare their own policy, independent of the government's. It looked suspiciously as though Major was happy for this to happen, as a way of getting round Ken Clarke's veto on a tougher Europe policy. What could Clarke do in the face of this semi-official revolt? He did nothing. No attempt was made by anyone to stop the

> "The Conservatives' inability to give a firm lead in Europe is damaging to our businesses. Their scare-mongering about what lies ahead in Europe is seriously counter-productive".

impression going out that this Tory Party would never give up the pound. For the first time in days, the news was dominated by a Tory problem, not Labour. But Major appeared not to regard it as a problem. He seemed content to let his party drift right, as it pleased, and to follow the lead of a junior minister because her direction suited him. At his morning press conference, Major was asked if he would guarantee Clarke the Chancellorship if the Tories won. He wouldn't.

As Blair said: "It did seem rather odd that the Prime Minister seemed to be giving his full backing to Mrs Browning, who is disagreeing with his policy, but giving less than full support to the Chancellor, who is the architect of that policy."

Blair was speaking at the launch of Labour's business manifesto. This was a remarkable event, simply by virtue of happening. It was held at the Institute of Chartered Accountants in the City of London. Terence Conran of Habitat, Gerry Robinson of Granada and the bookshop founder Tim Waterstone had front row seats. Although there had always been maverick businessmen supporting Labour, this was the most impressive gathering of company chiefs the party had put together.

One reason for this new mood among many businessmen - apart from the appeal of a likely winner - was Europe. As Robinson said: "The Conservatives' inability to give a firm lead in Europe is damaging to our businesses. Their scare-mongering about what lies ahead in Europe is seriously counter-productive."

Waterstone said Gordon Brown would be one of the finest Chancellors in years. "He has an almost apolitical sense of the need for stability in the economy."

Sarah McCartney, owner of a small business called Little Max, said she had voted for

Left: Tony Blair meets leading figures in the
City. Above: Tony Blair, Gordon Brown
and their aides discuss the presentation of
Labour's manifesto for business.

Margaret Thatcher in 1979, but now believed
Labour was the small business party. "They deal
with the real, everyday difficulties which face us
," she said, citing the Labour policy of forcing
big firms to pay debts promptly to small business. A few months earlier, Heseltine had boast-
ed that delaying the payment of debts had been
one of the secrets of his early survival in busi-

ness. The stark contrast with traditional Labour
policy launches was highlighted by a question
from Peter Riddell of The Times, who asked if
there was going to be a similar event with union
leaders.

"No," said Blair. Riddell said in his column
that he felt like a character in a Bateman cartoon
- the man who mentioned the unions.

UNION leaders had so far been conspicuous by their absence from the campaign, much to the Conservatives' irritation. But, like Europe, the union issue was still lurking in the deep.

The Sunday papers, egged on by Michael Heseltine, reported that the following week's Scottish TUC conference would discuss demands for a return to secondary picketing, the renationalisation of the railways and other horrors.

Heseltine said the conference agenda was "the most explosive document I have seen since this campaign began. This puts Mr. Blair at the mercy of the unions."

Apart from Heseltine's pantomime antics, the cuttings on Sunday, April 13, were not happy reading for Tony Blair. The Labour campaign was given rough reviews, the Tories' rave notices. There were tales of splits and backbiting, panic and disarray among the Labour high command. The Brown-Mandelson rift was resurrected and everyone from Cook to Blunkett via Prescott was alleged to have blown gaskets over the week's gaffes and U-turns.

Major told the Sunday Express: "I can taste the changing mood."

Blair travelled to Milton Keynes. A small crowd gathered at lunchtime for the unveiling of five new Labour posters - Income Tax Rates Will Not Rise, Class Sizes Will Be Smaller, NHS Waiting Lists Will Be Shorter, More Jobs For Young People, Young Offenders Will Be Punished.

There was more to this event than the usual poster launch. Blair had decided his campaign needed a new emphasis. It was time to accentuate the positive. He would do it by making an issue of Tory negative electioneering, building up Heseltine as the bogeyman of the campaign, a

> He strongly felt it was time to grasp the election by the scruff of the neck. He intended to shake people out of their cynicism. Tony would be "positive, positive, positive."

task in which Hezza needed little help.

Decisions to shift the emphasis of campaigning are always dangerous, not least because they are not normally taken by successful campaigns. They invite descriptions like "rethink", "re-launch" and, worse, "panic". Clearly the latter would be an exaggeration - even on the grimmest reading of the election so far, Labour's massive lead was being only slightly eroded by an untidy week on the defensive. Nevertheless, the Blair team was worried enough to run the risk of Tory gloating and announce a new tone to its campaign. Before letting the travelling media at its picnic of rolls and crisps for Sunday lunch, Alastair Campbell briefed in an office at the Milton Keynes international hockey centre. By coincidence, there was a notice on the wall setting out the kind of questions fashionable managers ask their staff - where are we? where are we going? how do we get there?

In Blair's case the answers were - ahead, to victory, by turning the tone of the Tory campaign into an issue and presenting himself as the man who wanted to talk seriously about the country's future. Campbell told his unenthused audience that Tony Blair strongly felt it was time to grasp the election by the scruff of the neck. He intended to shake people out of the media-inspired cynicism. Tony would be "positive, positive, positive" - hence the new posters, setting out his positive agenda.

Campbell had a go at the BBC for its tit-for-tat coverage. It was, of course, the BBC that had promoted the air traffic control controversy into the issue of the week. Campbell said few people were going to shift their vote on the future of air traffic control. Labour was confident that the dividing line between the parties would be between negative and positive campaigning.

Tony would be doing more "stump speeches". He would be more off the cuff. He would be "letting rip a bit more".

The buses headed for Birmingham. At the Hyatt Hotel, Blair dropped in on a drinks party for the travelling media. His appearance was overdue. The newspapers and broadcasting organisations were paying £7,500 for each season ticket on the Blair tour. Though the bus rides, the buns, the coddling and the smooth organisation, the phones and planes, the fruit and fizzy drinks were worth the money, a feeling had settled in that the lads were being short-changed on access to the leader. The Tories had been sharp enough to pick this up and Major had poked a good joke at Blair being kept away from journalists as if he had the plague. This all fed the Tory line that Blair was too much the creature of controllers.

However misplaced the charge , it was potentially damaging. Casual in an open-necked black shirt, Blair worked the room skilfully with beer in hand. He is good face-to-face. Reporters who had not met him before were impressed by the peculiar sensation that he was actually listening to them, interested in what they had to say. He seemed relaxed and his insistence that he was enjoying the campaign did not sound forced. His one frustration seemed to be the difficulty of reaching those voters who think all politicians are as bad as one another. But he was convinced that some of the people at his Q and A sessions were genuine non-believers who needed winning over.

The stay at the Hyatt was not entirely happy. When checking out next morning, the press party discovered they had been over-charged by £40 each - the difference to cover the cost of rooms for Blair's party. With the campaign in the doldrums, the cash-for-rooms scandal was an enjoyable sideshow.

As Blair began his education lecture at Birmingham University, there was furious muttering at the back of the hall as the press argued the details of "Hyattgate" with Lesley Smith, the press officer in charge of the reporters' bus.

This little cameo caught the flavour of the campaign. While Blair was setting out his serious agenda for change, the media was not concentrating. This was not the fault of the bus reporters - their job is always the day-to-day alarums, while political editors in London report on policy and the big picture of the election. But there was something characteristic of the campaign about Blair trying to talk about the choice facing the nation, while a petty squabble over hotel bills distracted the media.

Following pages: Tony Blair, arms outstretched, embraces the support of the crowd.

I T WAS not easy to rise above the political dog-fight. The low tone of the campaign suited the Conservatives. As Blair said at one of his regular question and answer sessions: "What the Tories will do is grind everybody down so that you say - what is the point?"

He himself was trying to get up on to the unoccupied high ground. His speech, 21 steps to a 21st Century education, was a densely packed brochure on Blair's Britain. For three years Blair and David Blunkett had been drafting a detailed prospectus and here he laid it all out, from the smaller classes pledge to new powers to suspend local authorities who were not running schools properly - "zero tolerance" for schools that failed their pupils.

The speech, to academics at Birmingham University, was delivered in Blair's best non-tubthumping style. That did not mean it lacked passion.

"Education is liberty," he declared, the neatest phrase he had yet found to express his conviction that better schooling was the key to the prosperous, united, more equal society he wanted. The speech deliberately kept party politics to a minimum - Blair even inserted a phrase conceding that the country's education failures did not start with this Tory government.

Major, by contrast, delivered a speech in Plymouth that devoted 16 out of 18 pages to attacking Labour.

"If they had a collective granny they would change her, provided there were votes in it," he said. He went for Blair personally and for the Blair family.

"What he wants for his children, he doesn't want for yours," said Major. He called Blair's appeal to the country "a shameless contract with hypocrisy."

Blair responded by again pointing out that he would be the first Prime Minister with his children at state schools. He refrained from adding

> The speech was delivered in Blair's best non-tubthumping style. This did not mean that it lacked passion.

that Major, having educated his own children at private schools, was certainly not offering the same to voters' children as he had wanted for his.

Major's main reason for being in the West Country was not education, but fish. The cuts in Britain's fishing quotas had long been one of the sharpest issues in the European debate - affecting real people and their livelihoods, unlike much of the arcane discussion about Europe. Major posed with Newlyn fisherman and said he would block agreement on the future of Europe at the Inter-Governmental Conference drawing up a new EU Treaty, unless Britain got a proper fish deal.

This was a wily defensive manoeuvre. Major knew that the following day Britain faced defeat on fish quotas at a meeting of European ministers, an awkward case of the real world intruding on the election. Major could not afford just to let his government look impotent in Luxembourg, he had to pre-empt and shape events. Hence his threat to the IGC, which would be culminating at a summit in Amsterdam a few weeks after the election. His aggressive tactics diverted attention from the inconvenient fact that nobody else's government but his had presided over the decline of British fishing, no other Prime Minister had failed to defend British fishing interests in Europe. Instead of debate focusing on Major's record, he succeeded in shifting it to what Labour would do, if Blair, rather than Major represented Britain in Amsterdam.

Blair had no hesitation in saying his government would also consider blocking the IGC. It was unheroic, but necessary. Blair was not prepared to let the Tories play the patriotic card and portray him as the poodle of Brussels. The time to strike a new British tone in Europe would have to wait until he was in power.

The dangers presented by Europe were underlined that night by the revelation that Dame Angela Rumbold, vice-chairman of the

*Student support
took many forms.*

Tory Party, was saying in her election address: "No to a single currency." As with the other Angela, Mrs. Browning, Major seemed content to let his party send the signal that he himself dared not give for fear of provoking Ken Clarke - that a Tory government would never take Britain into a single currency.

It was a dangerous game, but not just for Major. The obvious peril for him was a divided party. But Blair suspected Major was happy to take this risk in exchange for catching the Eurosceptic public mood.

"The Conservatives are being too clever by half here," Blair told his Tuesday morning Millbank press conference. "They almost want to parade their disunity. It isn't very smart. They can't fight for Britain's interests if they are fight-

ing themselves." Blair was in top form, as he continued to be throughout the day. The polls had steadied with Labour on average 17 points clear, and he was convinced the negative Tory tactics were a bad mistake. He was in such a confident mood that he even allowed himself to break his own number one rule.

At one of the day's campaign halts - the Queens Parade shopping centre in Crawley - he said: "The sun is out and in two weeks so will the Tories be."

He quickly remembered to add the usual qualifications about victory depending on "your support", but even the eternal warrior against complacency was having trouble disbelieving the biggest poll lead any challenger had ever held so close to polling day.

The great problem about Labour's lead was that the Tories looked so unlike a governing party that nobody was examining their policies. A fifth Tory term was so unreal it was impossible to frighten anyone about it. "You just focus on what it would be like if the Tories get re-elected," Blair told that day's Millbank press conference. "They would be like ferrets in a sack."

David Blunkett, sharing the platform with Blair, asked the kind of question of the Tories that was going unanswered. If they wanted a grammar school in every town, were they going to spend £7 million a time on new schools or were they going to turn existing comprehensives into grammars? Blunkett challenged every Tory candidate to say which good local school would be nominated as the one that would be excluding 80 per cent of the local children. Blair pointed out that a grammar in every town meant secondary moderns in every town.

The Tories had chosen Labour's minimum wage as their topic for the day. They rarely talked about their own policies, but were under-standably content to keep the election focused on Labour. There was little interest in the minimum wage, though.

Peter Lilley, the quietest of the Cabinet "Bastards", was asked if he could imagine himself backing a single currency.

He replied: "I have such a fertile imagination I can imagine almost anything."

This was a breath-takingly cheeky answer, almost poking fun at a wait-and-see policy which everyone knew he didn't believe in. It was not the reply of a government minister, but of a party power-broker looking ahead a short time to his role in the Tory leadership battle.

Unable to get the minimum wage running as an issue, Heseltine resorted to what was becoming the Tories' favourite weapon, Euan Blair.

Working himself up to theatrical indignation, the old ham thundered at Blair: "I can't stand the hypocrisy of a man who says that he would deny choice in the education system and then opts for choice for his own children. A man that will do that is not fit to discuss this country's education policy, let alone be Prime Minister".

There was no evidence that Labour policy would stop people like the Blairs sending their children across London to a church school of their choice.

As Blair said at Sussex University, his son "goes to a state school he could have gone to at any time in the last 30 years and will still be able to if there is a Labour victory. It is desperate Tory propaganda. Rather than focus on one child - my child - we should all be trying to see how we can raise the standards of millions of children who don't get the breaks they need."

The Brighton question and answer session was one of his best performances so far. Casting himself as the decent man trying to lift debate above a personal slanging match suited his style and his psychology. Indeed, Blair seemed to have settled into this role as Major had settled into being the 1992 underdog. All successful politicians have a style they are psychologically comfortable with. Major liked battling from behind. It suited Heseltine to be horrible. Blair was starting to thrive on the campaign trail as High Moral Tony. Increasingly, his chief concern was not so much the Tory attacks as the challenge of getting his moral seriousness through to a country made cynical by the Conservatives.

In particular, he seemed frustrated by the common view that he lacked principle and would do anything to get elected. During his Sussex University Q&A, there was sympathetic applause for a student called Alex, who asked if Blair cared more about Middle England's tax bills than the public services.

"Look," said Blair, as he often does. "It's not a sin to try to get elected, though I know people regard this as not the constitutional function of the Labour Party." It was the Tories who wanted the voters to be believe there was a choice on the centre-left between "a very principled Labour Party that was unelectable" and a Labour Party that was "electable but unprincipled".

A chaplain called Rob raised the problem of young people not bothering to vote. Blair shocked his audience by saying: "Even if you vote for a different party - do vote. People fought long and hard for the right to vote. I've very little time for people who say it makes no difference."

But millions did feel that way and Blair did have time for them. He was travelling thousands of miles to meet them, giving interview after interview to try to reach them. He had just logged up his 100th interview with national and local media in a fortnight.

April 15-16
THE REVOLT
OF THE
PIPSQUEAKS

BLAIR flew by helicopter from Sussex to Southampton, giving himself a long evening to write the speech he felt the campaign was badly in need of, about values and principles and political morality.

He was feeling confident. Before settling down to work, he did a phone-in on Sky TV and went for a drink with Jeremy Thompson, Sky's Blair-tour reporter, at a pub called the Royal Standard. Blair was struck by the enthusiasm he encountered in the pub, as he had been by the response of the crowd in Crawley. Politicians have a great capacity for self-delusion, but Blair was sure in this case his instincts were right. There really was a growing warmth for him and his party. However the media carped, he felt there was real interest in the election and a genuine mood for a new government. His staff noticed a big change in him on this crucial day. After a tense first fortnight, he was suddenly relaxed, as top performers are when they know they have got their game right.

Blair was writing in his room, 154, at the Grand Harbour Hotel, Southampton, when Alastair Campbell took a call from Charlie Whelan, press officer to Gordon Brown, but also much more than that. Whelan was one of the spin doctors with a seat at the "spin table", which dominated the war room at Labour's Millbank HQ. Those with seats at the "spin table", where hour-by-hour tactics were co-ordinated, were Peter Mandelson , David Hill, pollster Philip Gould, policy director Matthew Taylor, Campbell when in town, and Whelan.

Whelan is one of Westminster's premier gossips and therefore one of the party's most effective intelligence officers. He told Campbell he had heard a rumour that a Tory minister was about to

> When Campbell told his leader what was going on, Blair said, "They can't come back from this." It was the moment he knew he was going to be Prime Minister

break ranks on Europe. The name soon emerged. Tim Allan, Campbell's deputy, rang from the Commons press gallery to say John Horam, a junior health minister, was going on Newsnight to declare himself against the single currency.

When Campbell told his leader what was going on, Blair said: "They can't come back from this."

This was the moment when Tony Blair knew he was going to be Prime Minister. He knew the election was won. There was a knock on the door: Jim Naughtie of the BBC had come to record an interview for the following morning's Today programme. Blair and Naughtie agreed that with events moving so swiftly they should do it in the morning. Blair didn't bother to watch Newsnight, but got on with his speech.

It was soon clear that another minister, education under-secretary James Paice, would be named in the next day's Times, along with Horam. Both were putting out election addresses that broke government policy on the single currency.

These were very junior people - that was the point. When the pipsqueaks feel safe to rebel, leadership is coming to an end. Central Office was soon signalling there would be no sackings. It was a humbling admission of Major's lost authority.

More than 100 candidates had by now declared themselves against the single currency, including Sir Marcus Fox, chairman of the Tory backbenchers' 1922 committee. His election address was handed to correspondents by Central Office, confirming the impression of the party command as a Euro-sceptic HQ. It looked as though the Tory Party was not going to bother to wait for defeat before disintegrating.

Blair said in his Naughtie interview that the

Relaxed in the sunshine: Tony Blair's confidence was growing by the day.

Helicopters played an important part in an efficient, modern, fast-moving campaign.

ministers' revolt was a defining moment in the campaign. But he was not going to publicly admit his certainty of victory. He and Campbell instead hinted at concern that this outbreak of Euro-scepticism might even help the Tories by exploiting public doubts about the single currency. This was the line from Central office too. The Tories claimed to be getting a good response on the doorstep now that Europe was the issue. Labour's polling instantly showed this line to be mere spin-doctoring. Division and weak leadership were doing much more harm than any good done by moving rightwards.

Another pipsqueak, Transport Minister John Watts, went on the World At One to say he would leave the government if it recommended the single currency. Ken Clarke had been due to appear, but didn't. He was drifting out of the Tory campaign. Brian Mawhinney squirmed in Clarke's place. He defended Horam on the grounds that he was merely expressing his personal opposition to the single currency, while confirming that in his ministerial capacity he thought the government had the "right line". It is only slightly to parody Mawhinney's argument to say that ministers were free to oppose government policy, provided they said they supported it.

With his campaign in crisis, it was time for emergency action from Major.

An hour before his morning press conference, he sat down with Clarke, Mawhinney and Gillian Shephard, the scheduled line-up for that day's platform. Major told them he intended to scrap their planned presentation on jobs - official unemployment was due to fall that day - and instead give an unscripted defence of his wait-and-see Euro policy.

Depending on how the single currency works out - or doesn't - Major's performance at Central office with his party in revolt may go down as his finest moment. His place in history - to which he referred, revealingly - may be as the man who stopped a crazed Tory Party driving Britain irrevocably to the fringes of Europe. For all his twisting and turning on Europe, Major did keep the options open for the head of a more coherent government.

Major set out both the advantages and disadvantages of the Euro and some of his audience felt he put the case for the single currency more eloquently than the case against.

"Can anybody honestly put their hand on their heart and say they know what the outcome would be if we were to decide now?"

Of course, scores of his candidates were doing just that, with the tacit support of much of the Cabinet.

Major talked of the foreign investment in Britain that might be jeopardised by isolation from the Euro.

"Can anyone be certain that that huge flood of inward investment would continue?"

Against joining, he said it would be a catastrophe "beyond calculation" if Britain signed up to a single currency that failed. He admitted, more honestly than he had so far had the courage to, that he was "scarred" by the experience of joining the Euro's predecessor, the ERM, and seeing it fail.

Had he spoken this frankly and with such feeling before, he and his party might not be in their dire position, nor might politicians in general be held in such low esteem.

Now he appealed to his party: "Whether you agree with me or disagree with me, like me or loathe me, don't bind my hands when I am negotiating for the British nation".

He clasped his hands together in an explosion of flashguns, to emphasise this plea for a free hand.

It was a shocking thing to hear a Prime Minister admitting that part of his party loathed him. This is not how leaders speak unless they feel, deep down, they will soon be free of exasperating followers.

It was the first time Major had set out so firmly the case for refusing to close options, while remaining deeply suspicious of the whole Euro project. This was, by now, Labour's policy too. Blair and Robin Cook had seen this coming and wanted to be sure that the Conservatives could not turn their difficulties against Labour with scare-mongering about a new government blindly joining the Euro.

Major's dignified, cogent expression of the cross-party consensus - though he wouldn't ever call it that - impressed his audience. Jon Snow of Channel Four told him it was a shame it couldn't be broadcast.

Major decided it should. Instead of setting off straight away for a visit to Teesside with Lady Thatcher, he re-shot a tidied-up version of his press conference reply, direct to camera, to be shown in place of that night's planned party political broadcast on jobs. Sadly, this meant keeping Thatcher waiting for an hour at Teesside Airport.

She was not the ideal companion on such a day, having already made clear her opposition to the single currency. When Major finally arrived, the two of them had a long talk on his bus. They could be seen sharing a table. Perhaps she had needed no telling, but when they emerged she seemed oddly deaf to questions about the Euro.

Visiting a factory in Cardiff, Blair said he felt sorry for Major.

"You can't run a political party like this," he said. Despite his sympathy, Blair added a point aimed at Euro-sceptic voters about the Tories: "They couldn't represent Britain properly in Europe. They just couldn't do it."

Major looked weary on his television broadcast. His performance was not quite so good as at the press conference. His tone was that of a man mentally packing his suitcase. Never had a Prime Minister had to go on air during an election campaign and , in effect, appeal to the country to back him despite his party. It felt like the end - with his party going to pieces, the outgoing Prime Minister had only his dignity left to play for.

The following morning, on the Today programme, Michael Portillo refused to say anything on the single currency that might damage his chances of leading a party that was accelerating his way. Throughout the day, he politely dodged the question - could you imagine ever supporting a single currency? To answer Yes would damage his chances in the leadership election he hoped soon to be fighting, but 'No' would gravely harm the government's chances in the election ministers were supposed to be contesting now.

Tony Blair told his morning press conference: "There are two Conservative Parties fighting this election. I think neither will be elected."

THE speech that Blair was writing when the decisive news from the Tory battlefront first arrived was even more important now that the election looked won and lost. It was time to set out the principles that would guide the new government. Blair spent much of the night re-drafting. He wanted it just right and very personal. Though all the policies and beliefs in the speech were familiar to Blair-watchers, he wanted them pulled together in a single theme that would convince a sceptical country of his sense of purpose.

He chose a phrase that had often been tucked away in his speeches, The Decent Society. Blair defined it this way: "It will be a new Labour government's task to rebuild Britain as one nation, where every individual has a stake in its future, where we treat poverty and unemployment not as problems we shut out or ignore, but as intolerable in any decent society true to the best of British values."

This key sentence gathered up the strands of Blairism. Decency was a very Blair word, with its moral overtones. "Best of British" emphasised his conviction that Labour's compassion was closer to the national character than hard-hearted Toryism. One Nation was a shrewd piece of political pilfering from the Tory left, a favourite phrase to suggest that Labour could create a more equal society without threatening ex-Tory voters.

It was characteristic of Blair to have the word "individual" in his core statement. He believed Labour had crucially lost touch with individual aspirations in the 1970s and 80s. The way to reclaim personal aspiration was to offer everyone a "stake" in society. This did not mean, as the Tories caricatured it, a return of trade union excess. He meant that the unemployed, the poor and the neglected must all feel they too have

> "A decent society judges itself by the condition of the weak as well as the strong."
>
> It was as good a definition of socialism in the age of the soundbite as you'd wish for.

something to gain from the country's success, otherwise society would fracture and crime would breed in the wasteland.

This desire to bring the excluded minority in without redistributing prosperity away from the middle-classes was the key to Blairism. It had to be done without higher tax, or the middle classes would not stand for it. But that did not mean writing off the poor. It meant finding new ways of lifting them from poverty. When Blair said poverty and unemployment were intolerable, it was more than a statement of his political morality, important though that was. He believed he had the policies to deliver this high aim, like the windfall tax and, in the longer run, his education crusade.

His emphasis on conquering poverty was welcome to colleagues who had longed for him to stress the commitment to the poor which they knew he had, but which he had been shy of expressing.

"A Decent Society judges itself by the condition of the weak as well as the strong," said Blair. It was as good a definition of socialism in the age of the soundbite as you could wish for.

His Decent Society was about "security for all". He rejected the division between the well-off, the "anxious majority" and the underclass. Prosperity would not last if it was reserved for the few. A bigger wage packet could not guarantee security from crime or a decent health and education service. Insecurity and division had undermined the national sense of purpose. Society could not be strong when one household in five had no wage-earner.

This was not the speech of a secret Tory. It was the speech of a man who wanted to take the Tories' lopsided economic success and build on it a "united nation" - as he called it - that any Labour leader would have been proud of.

Though he went through the manifesto pledges that would deliver this united nation, he

stressed throughout that his government was not just about the policies it would implement, but about the change of culture it would bring.

The Tories wanted to drag everyone down to their level so that the voters concluded that politicians were all the same. They wanted the country to believe that things could never be better. But this was the politics of despair. Labour, he said, would "restore the moral dimension of British government".

Even the footsore bus party, over-familiar with Blair's themes after listening to him daily for what seemed like forever, came out of the Harbour Lights Cinema, Southampton, saying with an air of slight surprise that it had been a great speech.

Inevitably, though, it was given less coverage than the Tory civil war. When he was asked about this, Blair said he was of course happy for the Conservative collapse to be copiously reported, but he was "deeply frustrated" at the difficulty of making himself heard above the noise of the Tory battles.

Well aware of the charge that he stood for nothing and was the creature of his spin doctors, Blair was much attracted by the idea of speaking off the cuff, as Campbell had said at the start of

this crucial week. Blair was already doing this when his bus pulled up in town squares and he was getting into a habit of adding unscripted finales to his more formal speeches.

In Edinburgh, he went further. Ideally, he would have liked to deliver the whole speech unscripted. But the media likes an advance copy to file before deadline - by the time he finished in Edinburgh it would be after 8pm, too late to catch the first editions of the morning papers. Blair's staff circulated a short passage on the NHS, warning that if the Tories got back they would regard it as a "licence to kill" the health service. He would start with this and move into the unknown.

He departed from his normal preparations. Like any politician , Blair has speech writers on whose work he builds his final text. Normally, he tries out his best lines on advisors like Alastair Campbell, Pat McFadden and Tim Allan, asking what they think. This time he asked his staff to leave him in his hotel room for 90 minutes before going on stage at the Usher Hall, so that he could "focus himself". Only Cherie was with him.

The plan was that, when the time came to depart from the prepared text, he would walk

Time for the elderly. Pensions played a vital and controversial part in Labour's campaign.

Leader at the gate: Tony and Cherie Blair out on the streets of South London.

away from the podium and microphone, to the front of the stage. He had a small personal mike clipped to his lapel, so that his voice would carry to the 1,600 people in the three-tiered concert hall.

At first it worked well. Labour was the party of aspiration and ambition, he said, but was different from the Tories because it believed that ambition was not just for the people at the top.

"Everyone should leave school and be able to say - I have something to do with my life." Labour wanted a "nation of all the talents", a phrase he had not used before and a very good one to describe his all-inclusive One Nation economy. He wanted a country with enough confidence to let its young people "flourish and bloom".

An unpleasant crackling interrupted him and, midway through a sentence about two Tory recessions, the lapel mike broke down. This was

a nasty moment. The obvious thing would be to return to the microphone at the podium and for a second he considered it. But to scuttle back to safety would have been to invite ridicule of his attempt at spontaneity. His failure - not the mike's - would have become the story. What a gloriously catty sketch it would have made. He had to go on.

Raising his voice to reach the back stalls on the top tier, he said: "We are going to make our voices carry on May 1, all the way through the ..."

Presumably "country", but the cheering drowned his unamplified voice.

The Tories accused of him of doing anything to get elected, but "I want to be elected because I believe I can make this country better, I want to be elected because for 18 years I have been a doer, not a sayer and I came into politics to get things done." Despite his acoustic handicap, or perhaps because of it, he was at last worked up about his desire to serve and to change the coun-

try. "A woman said to me the other day - tell me, could things ever really change? I said to her: things will change if you want them to change. If you have the faith to make the change."

There was a real sense of a polished performer breaking out of the inevitable packaging of modern politics.

"If I carry on like this, I am going to lose my voice," he said.

"The Conservatives want to frighten people. Fear has been their weapon, terrifying people out of the prospect of change.

"I say to you - fear may be the Tory weapon, but it is hope that is the weapon of today's Labour Party, hope that our children's future will

be better. We will make this country better. We will build a country we can be proud of again. It can happen. It will happen."

The standing ovation was not a duty. In the TV age, public speaking is a dead art and the audience seemed delighted to have watched the ultimate telegenic political star have a go at the real thing and pull it off. When Cherie joined him on stage, he couldn't help looking a little relieved it was over and quite excited by the response. It was a better Scottish reception than the Glasgow media had given him a fortnight before.

Looking forward: Tony Blair visits the Christopher Hatton School in London.

THE Edinburgh Evening News quoted Malcolm Rifkind: "All the Cabinet are a single happy family." This was not quite true. Major had thrown his family into fresh disarray over Europe, by promising a free vote on the single currency.

Major is a strange man. There are many Majors. He changes day by day, sometimes hour by hour. You can sometimes see the various Majors jostling one another.

On Wednesday April 16, we saw Major the statesman, who told his press conference: "I have to answer to my conscience and my nation and history."

But, having stood up to the Eurosceptics, he promptly caved in to them on April 17. His promise of a free vote was given casually in response to a question from the needle-sharp Elinor Goodman of Channel Four.

Accused of making up policy as he went along, Major said: "I didn't suddenly announce it. If you had asked me a couple of years ago I probably would have told you".

But he hadn't told his Chancellor, or his deputy. Ken Clarke did not bother to conceal his surprise at this rightward policy lurch. He told the World At One he hadn't known about it because he had been out of town, in Bristol and in his Nottinghamshire constituency - a new definition of being all over the place.

Pressed on his colleagues' ignorance, Major said: "If I had replied to the question and said 'I'm frightfully sorry, that's a very interesting question but I'd better go and ask Ken Clarke or Joe Bloggs or someone else before I give you an answer' - that may be the way the Labour Party operates , it's not the way I operate."

This was a sentence rich in confusion. For instance, only a week before, Major had been pillorying Tony Blair for operating precisely in the way he described - not consulting colleagues, but

The ad had a huge impact, confirming the suspicion that Heseltine was a high-class advertising copywriter who had wandered into government instead of a pet food account.

inventing policy as he went along. Now this was OK. Worse than that, though, was the confusion of his Chancellor with Joe Bloggs. It was a very peculiar idea that a Prime Minister should give his Chancellor no more consideration than Mr. Bloggs on the biggest economic policy question of the age. Major seemed to have got a little carried away with the notion that he was offering himself rather than his party for re-election.

The depth of his incompetence was revealed by the difficulties he caused for Michael Heseltine. Say what you like about Heseltine, he is a pro. He does not often make mistakes, but now he did and it was Major's fault.

He too was unconsulted about his leader's instant policymaking, but went off on the day's travels under the impression that the free vote was a hint rather than a pledge. When Charlie Lee Potter of the PM programme suggested it was now a commitment, Heseltine ranted at her for misquoting and grossly distorting what the Prime Minister had said. Unhappily for Hezza, Major had indeed hardened his hint into a pledge by saying, during a visit to Ellesmere Port, that there "must" be a free vote. But no-one had told the Deputy Prime Minister.

When the top three people in a government don't know what each other are doing, it is time for them to take a rest. But the long Tory holiday was two weeks off. They had to keep going and the only way to do that was to get more vicious.

Heseltine had already had just the idea. How about portraying Blair as a boy seeking a man's job? How about an advert showing a little Blair on a giant Helmut Kohl's knee? Heseltine had come up with this a couple of weeks before during a strategy session and provoked even the funereal Mawhinney to giggle at his quick sketch of big Helmut and little Tony. The ever-willing, ever-cynical Maurice Saatchi had oblig-

Thousands of hands to shake as time ticks away to polling day.

ed by taking the idea away and turning it into an ad that was now ready for Major's sanction. Those who accused Blair of being the creature of his spin doctors seemed oddly blind to the regular presence at Major's press conferences of his private sector surgeons, Lord Saatchi, Lord Gummer and Sir Tim Bell. They liked to stand all in a row beneath their slogan "Britain is Booming - Don't Let Labour Blow It."

The "Kohl's Knee" ad had a huge impact, confirming the suspicion that Heseltine was in fact a high-class advertising copywriter who had wandered into government instead of working on a soft drinks or pet food account.

Labour called the ad "pathetic", but it was worse than that. It showed how shamelessly the Tories were prepared to appeal to the worst side of the British character in a desperate search for votes. The giant Kohl was a pitch for the floating hooligan.

It was one way of distracting from Tory disunity. But the divide could not be concealed.

Margaret Thatcher, on the loose without

Major at her side, was asked during a visit to an Essex supermarket whether she supported the single currency.

"My goodness, no," she replied.

Her old adversary, Geoffrey Howe, denounced the Kohl ad. More ominously, Clarke made sure the newspapers learned that he was unhappy. The Financial Times reported: "The Chancellor took the unusual step of authorising one of his aides to disclose that he had 'not been consulted in advance'".

Unlike his fellow pro-European, Michael Heseltine, Clarke still felt some things were more important than the desperate hunt for votes. But he looked very lonely as the pipsqueaks towed the Tory Party further and further from the mainland.

The idea that Europe posed a threat to Britain was "paranoid nonsense", said Clarke at the Tory Party's Saturday press conference at Central Office. He was probably the only person on the premises who felt that way.

HOW seriously did Major think he could win? How much did he really want to win, with much of his party, by his own admission, loathing him?

He gave a strange interview to The Times at No 10 on Saturday morning, April 19, which read less like a campaign interview than the first interview in retirement.

He offered to give Tony Blair advice on how to handle other European leaders and spoke of those leaders like a man who would not be dealing with them again, referring to them as "those so-and-sos". Reading the interview, it was hard to resist the feeling that Major would be glad to hand over the intractable problem of Europe. But how would Blair handle it?

The interview was published on Monday morning. Blair's "grid" for the campaign had always shown this as the day when he would give his main set-piece speech on Europe. On the face of it, the timing was perfect.

However, there was a yearning in much of the Labour Party to hear him talking about anything but Europe. This, it was felt, was the Tory agenda and it was time for Tony Blair to start talking about Labour's agenda, to Labour's core voters.

"They don't think we've got anything to say to them," said one Blair admirer who felt the Labour leader was paying too little attention to long-standing Labour voters.

"I'm afraid there'll be a low turn-out because we're not doing enough to tell our people that we'll make a difference. If there is a low turn-out, the Tories will be there in the polling booths - they always are."

There was a dilemma at the heart of the Blair campaign. The more he reassured ex-Tories they had nothing to fear, the more Labour's tradition-

"We can do it because we have courage and faith in ourselves. Over the next eight or nine days the future of this country will be decided.

Have confidence, have strength, have faith."

al support feared he had nothing to offer. His carefully-costed programme of deliverable commitments was meant to solve this dilemma, by showing that a realistic manifesto could "make a start" without "promising the earth". The trouble with this strategy was that the Tories could belittle it and left-of-centre commentators sneer. There was a peculiar alliance between fashionable metropolitan opinion formers, who refused to believe in change that did not increase the tax on their comfortable incomes, and Conservatives who wanted the country to believe that an electable Labour leader must by definition be unprincipled.

The combined message from these two very different sources contributed to an odd mood of disenchanted expectation of victory. The Conservatives played on this mood cleverly with their constant repetition of the charge that Blair would say anything to win. Major was not so naive as to think that negative campaigning repelled voters. That was what the voters said, but not how they responded. He knew he was touching a public nerve when he attacked Blair for "shifting and shuffling and shifting again" and for being "carried away with his own propaganda".

Before tackling this problem, Blair had first to go ahead with his Europe speech. There was still a job of reassurance to do here - there was disturbing evidence that the voters still didn't know Labour was promising a referendum. To an audience of diplomats in Manchester, Blair said he would not hesitate to oppose a European superstate and would "have no truck" with a fudged single currency.

He was content to have this speech portrayed as Eurosceptic - the risk of being depicted as the defender of Brussels against British interests was not worth running, when up against a cornered Conservative Party. This danger was

highlighted within hours by Jacques Santer, President of the European Commission, who made a crassly timed pronouncement that there was no alternative to further European integration. The Tories were delighted, saying Santer had reinforced their fears. Blair could not afford to be trapped into siding with Santer, hence his coolness towards the great European project.

But there was a pro-European message wrapped up in Blair's sceptical speech.

"I am a British patriot," he said. "I will always put the interests of my country first. But the Britain of my vision is not a Britain turning its back on the world - narrow, shy, uncertain."

There was a bottom line here, for those who wanted to find it, that he would not allow the sceptics to turn Britain into an offshore island too frightened of Europe to play the leading role it deserved. It may tactically suit Blair the candidate to protect his flank against a Eurosceptic Tory campaign, but Blair the Prime Minister would not allow the sceptics to dictate his agenda. To his detractors, Blair's behaviour on Europe was a typical piece of shifting and shuffling. To his supporters, it was the kind of

manoeuvring made necessary by unscrupulous opponents, whose defeat had to be the only priority now that polling day was so close.

Nevertheless, Blair recognised that his efforts to reassure middle Britain might rebound if he did not answer the charge of standing for nothing. Though he felt he had answered the charge, he knew the mass of voters had not heard. Unless he could make the public hear him, he could not tackle his two most dangerous opponents, apathy and cynicism.

Before a big, enthusiastic crowd in Chester, he took a swipe at the media: "When they say there is no enthusiasm for this election, I say - look at these crowds. There is enthusiasm for change in this country. People do want change. We can do something for the people of this country, but we can only do it if people are going to come out and vote on 1 May."

It was one thing to enthuse crowds of shoppers and party members, but his point had not got through to the opinion-forming classes in London. The best place to reach them was the London Press Club, whose annual lunch Blair

Tony and Cherie Blair aboard a Virgin train with Richard Branson.

Getting the strategy right: Tony Blair and press secretary Alastair Campbell.

addressed on Tuesday, April 22.

Politely, he complained to an audience of editors and columnists of a "conspiracy against understanding", especially in the broadcasters' coverage of the campaign. He talked about a "constant battle between stories and issues - stories happen all the time, but there is an underlying discussion of the issues which often doesn't get much play in the media".

He said he had been frustrated by the difficulty of getting coverage for his three speeches in Birmingham, Southampton and Edinburgh. "It means some of the passion and conviction of a different vision gets pushed to one side".

He said: "It is quite difficult for the public to understand there are issues of considerable

moment that are going to be decided".

This was not just the last general election of the 20th Century, but the last election fought on 20th Century ideology and politics. The best way to explain what he meant was to put it personally.

"I am modern man," he said. "I am a product of my generation, that has grown up without the easy simplicities of left and right of the past century".

The political divisions of the first half of the century were "not relevant" to the modern world.

"People say - if you don't stand for the past, you stand for nothing," he said. "That is nonsense. We stand for strong values and principles. I do believe in a fair deal for ordinary people. I can read a speech of Keir Hardie and recognise exactly what I believe. I can do the same with Attlee and Wilson. What I would not recognise are the prescriptions. The liberation of the Labour Party from outdated prescriptions, to allow those values to take root in the modern world, is of enormous benefit."

This election was "being fought on the old terms". But if he was successful "the next election will be fought on a different basis".

This was a large claim, that went unnoticed. What he meant was that, by the time he had been in power for a few years, all the old arguments about the state and the market, about privatisation, about tax and spending - all of it would be irrelevant in the new politics he would create. He would do it by turning Labour into a business-friendly party that insisted on profit being used for the public good, a party that showed greater equality could be achieved without punitive taxation, a party which showed that a prosperous economy is more likely to thrive if the poor are given the chance to earn their fair share of the nation's wealth. But that was not a story. It was an issue - a very big issue - and therefore pushed to one side.

His main weapon against cynicism was by now the unscripted speech. In Stevenage he strode to the front of the stage and said: "Last time I did this the mike packed up. Do they deserve five more years, then?" "No-o-o". "I'm going to tell you this evening what is going to change under a Labour government.

"First off, we will re-build the NHS as a decent public service. Who do you trust with the NHS? I'll tell you another thing that will change. (Cheers) You're getting into it now. We spend £3 billion in this country subsidising low pay. I say, let's introduce a proper minimum wage."

He went on through the list of pledges, familiar to the political classes, but not to the casual voter.

"These are all good reasons to come out and vote Labour on May 1st. But there is a bigger vision that I want to share with you tonight. When people see television broadcasts which are all tit for tat, there is no sense that this is an election about the soul of this country. This is a landmark election.

"I believe in New Labour. For me, New Labour is not some public relations gimmick, or some salesman's patter. I believe in the Labour Party and its values, but they must be applied in a different way from our ancestors.

"I am a modern man, from the rock and roll generation - The Beatles, colour TV, that's my generation.

"My ideals are simple. Women should have the choice to go out to work or stay home.

"I believe in a society where we loathe and abhor racialism. I believe in a society where those that hassle and abuse the elderly and vulnerable deserve to be punished.

"Those are simple attitudes, but they don't fit easily into the political simplicities of earlier political times."

This was a popular version of the broadsheet address he had given at the London Press Club.

"These are the attitudes of my generation. These are the things Labour stands for. These are the things that this election is about.

"We can do it if we have courage and faith in ourselves, because the only weapon they know is fear.

"So, my friends, over the next eight or nine days, the future of this country will be decided. Have confidence. Have strength. Have faith."

*Following pages: Supporter-in-Chief
Cherie Blair shares a private moment
with her husband as he works
on a speech.*

April 23-25
BARE-FACED
LIAR

AND then the polls moved, again. Or one poll did. As the capacity audience spilled out of the Stevenage Arts and Leisure Centre, Labour staff badgered journalists for news of ICM in The Guardian, rumoured to have the lead down to single figures. The rumour was true. The lead was a hair-raising five - 42 points to 37.

Major was for the first time ahead of Blair as the best PM. It looked as though Blair's fears about Europe may be born out. For Eurosceptics, here was a sign that they had been right all along to clamour for a rightwing, nationalistic campaign - the candidates' revolt had washed Major out into some clear blue water and the tide might be turning.

There was nothing for Blair to do but wait for a trend. A single poll meant nothing. Even that night, there was news of Gallup putting Labour's lead sharply up, to 21 points.

When the ICM poll came up at his Wednesday morning press conference, Blair said: "As I always say, there is only one poll that counts and that is the one on election day."

There was no Tory trend. That evening, Channel Four's Harris poll put Labour on 50, the Tories on 31. More interestingly, it showed that half the population was not yet committed. Here surely was the key to the mystery of the polls. Nobody believed Labour was 20-odd points ahead, or that its lead had been dramatically cut. Something unmeasurable was going on in the dying days of Tory Britain. Deep down, people wanted a change and felt Labour probably deserved office - but they weren't sure.

A cautious country was bound to hesitate before committing itself to a party so long out of power. What was going on, as polling day approached, was a bit like last night nerves before a wedding. A number of voters would balk at going down the aisle, but most would go through with it, despite liking Blair a little less

Major accused Blair of getting into the gutter. Blair was certainly not on high ground. He was focusing the public mind on the perils of a Tory victory.

since seeing so much of him these last few weeks. As the polls steadied, they put Blair back in front of Major personally.

In this unsettled, not quite committed atmosphere, people had to be reassured, day after day, and shown the rewards they would get from a Labour government. Blair had long talked about his three Rs - Labour must Reassure, Reward and Remind (of the Tory record). This formula was laid down in Labour's "war book", the lean, mean battle plan on which the campaign was based.

Someone had leaked a version of the war book to Conservative Central Office, complete with brown envelope. Brian Mawhinney had held it back for a rainy day - there was nothing in it that alert observers of Labour's tactics could not have written down for themselves. But Mawhinney knew how much the media likes a good leak. It would grab the headlines at a moment of necessity.

He decided to play the war book now, partly because Labour's theme for the day was getting a good response. Blair had devoted his morning press conference on April 23 to an announcement that Labour would spend some of the proceeds from the national lottery on health and education projects. It was the kind of detailed, practical policy that Blair liked - very much what he had in mind when he talked about his second R, rewarding people for voting Labour. Here was a nicely deliverable piece of populism that showed Labour had something positive to offer.

It went well on the lunchtime news. By the evening news, Mawhinney had muscled into the headlines with his leaked war book, which he denounced as proof that Labour was running the most cynical campaign ever, with its smears plotted months in advance.

It would have been very strange if Labour had not had a well-prepared strategy for its third R, reminding the voters of the dangers of voting

96

Tory. This had proved unexpectedly difficult, because nobody took a fifth Tory term seriously. With Labour so far ahead, it seemed a little eccentric to even wonder what the Tories would do. Nobody was interested in closely examining policies that were unlikely to be implemented.

It took the Tories themselves finally to get the Tory threat to the top of the bulletins. They did it by over-reacting to the charge that they would abolish the state pension. It happened, all of a sudden, on the Thursday afternoon a week before polling day.

There was no immediately obvious reason for the strength of their reaction on that afternoon. The pensions threat was not even Labour's theme for the day. Blair's coup that morning was producing Alan Sugar, head of Amstrad and owner of Tottenham Hotspur, as his latest business backer - describing Blair as "aggressive, hungry for it ... on balance I think the guy can do it".

At the press conference, Blair had stood before a list of his own pledges, alongside a list of what the Tories would do. The last on the Tory list was "abolishing the state pension".

This was not a new line of attack. Stopping the Tories abolishing the state pension had been a line guaranteed to raise a cheer in every street corner speech. The Tories had not responded, but now they called a mid-afternoon press conference at which Stephen Dorrell accused Blair of "bare-faced despicable lies". He read this from a prepared statement, to ensure that nobody thought there was anything accidental or bungled about the strength of his language. The Tories were, linguistically, going nuclear.

The reason for this massive response was mounting alarm at Central Office that the pension issue was causing trouble on the doorsteps. Labour's drip-drip accusation had got the voters

Tony Blair makes a point to journalists travelling on the battlebus.

worried. Rather than put out a well-argued rebuttal that would die a death on the inside pages, the Conservatives decided to nuke Blair. They got the top-of-the-news, front-page coverage they wanted.

It was a risky move. If they could force Blair to retreat or even waver, it would be a double direct hit on his integrity and his bottle. But what if the public was inclined to believe Blair, or at least distrust Tory propaganda more than Labour's?

Far from retracting, Blair looked delighted. Appearing solo on the BBC's Question Time, he said: "I am not letting the Tories get away without proper scrutiny of a fifth term."

He reminded viewers of all the things the Tories had slipped through without proper scrutiny - doubling VAT in 1979, the poll tax in 1987, VAT on fuel in 1992.

He was given a hard time at his Friday morning press conference, but he stood his ground. He wanted the fifth term to be the issue, even if he had to take some flak for the way he made it so. Elections are not won by Queensbury Rules.

Major accused Blair of getting into the gutter. Blair was certainly not on the high ground. But he was doing what he had long wanted to do as the campaign approached its climax. He was focusing the public mind on the perils of a Tory victory. He had always said that he couldn't believe the people would go through with it when confronted with the prospect of waking on May 2 with Major safe in Downing Street.

Major seemed genuinely angered by the pensions scare. He was unable to see the historical neatness of Labour's tactics. The Tories had won in 1992 by frightening the voters with phoney figures about Labour's tax plans. The pensions scare was Labour's revenge. Though it carried the danger of dragging Labour down to the Tories' level, veterans of '92 could not help enjoying Major's fury. One of the oddest things about Major is that he really cannot accept that his 1992 campaign - the tax bombshell, the pledge not to extend VAT - was dishonest. He can see nothing wrong with saying what he did and then himself raising taxes more sharply than he had said Labour would. Nor can he see why nobody accepts that he really didn't have any plans for extending VAT - the need just happened to arise shortly thereafter.

He believes his Honest John propaganda. He had written in one speech that week, in Aberdeen: "Look in my eyes and know this. I will always deal fair and true by this great nation."

He didn't actually say the words - not because he hadn't the nerve, but because he was forever infuriating his spin doctors and scriptwriters by not bothering with the best lines after he agreed them. His "look in my eyes" passage was nevertheless widely covered - the text having been filed in advance. This passage was an accurate reflection of the man's self-image. He actually expected the voters to trust him.

Major's self-memory is highly selective. He is able to convince himself he has been fair and true by this great nation. He has never understood that much of this great nation has concluded from his behaviour that all politicians are liars, which may be his saddest legacy.

Now he was calling Blair a liar. The pensions episode was not just a low point in the campaign, but in democratic politics. There has to be a better was of fighting elections than this. But the Tories could hardly make a legitimate complaint about having their own low tactics turned against them.

THE 1997 election was a marathon and Tony Blair prepared himself physically as well as politically. He worked out every morning at home with weights. He made time for two games of tennis a week, right through the campaign.

This was the simple explanation of the energy that puzzled and slightly appalled the exhausted media who travelled with him.

He joked with them one day: "You're looking a bit jaded, guys".

It was one of the few things he said all campaign that went unquestioned.

One day when I wearily asked him how come he looked so fresh, he said: "I never felt fitter in my life."

He got up every morning at six, worked out, had a bath (never a shower) and woke Cherie with a cup of tea. He listened to the 6.30am headlines on the BBC's Today programme. Euan, 13, is , apart from his father, the earliest riser in the Blair family, but Nicky, 11, and Kathryn, 9, were also up early enough to see Dad, except when he made overnight stops.

The day's work began at 7am, when Alastair Campbell arrived. If proximity is the key to influence, there is no doubt who was the key influence on Blair during the campaign. Blair and Campbell would immediately sit down to talk by conference telephone to the team at Millbank - Gordon Brown, Peter Mandelson, David Hill, Jo Moore (Hill's deputy), Jonathan Powell (Blair's chief of staff, a former diplomat and brother of Sir Charles, who had been Thatcher's chief foreign affairs advisor) and David Milliband (Blair's head of policy). This was not an exclusive club. Sometimes others would take part, like Brian Wilson, the sharpwitted frontbencher whose skills as a journalist had made him a lead-

The United manager, Alex Ferguson, told him he was 4-2 up with 20 minutes to go. His team would be waiting for their opponents to make mistakes. "Then we kill 'em".

ing player in the party's press operation.

Much of this meeting would be devoted to an overnight update, a look at the theme of the day and a brainstorming on the questions likely to be faced at the morning press conference. It was a well-drilled operation, to ensure that Blair was never caught off guard. No leader likes saying: I don't know.

For instance, when Clare Short said something about drugs on a midnight talk show that the media was half-interested in making mischief with, Blair was able to close the potential problem down at his press conference because he had already seen the transcript prepared by the monitoring unit that worked round the clock. It was going to take more than getting up early to catch out Tony Blair.

After his 7am consultations with Millbank, Blair would have breakfast amid the before-school comings and goings familiar to any father preparing for work in the midst of a young family. Cherie's mother Gale stayed for the duration, to maintain some stability in the children's lives with their parents away so much. There is plenty of Blair and Booth family living around about in London, including Tony's brother Bill and sister Sarah and Cherie's sister Lyndsay.

The red Jaguar, loaned by the company for the campaign, would take Blair and Campbell from Islington to Millbank for the 8.30am press conference, which always opened with a short video of the latest scenes from the Blair tour and the campaign theme song, Things Can Only Get Better.

When the 200-plus journalists decamped from Millbank to Smith Square for Major's 9.15 press conference, Blair would normally have another tactical meeting, this time just with Brown, Mandelson and Campbell.

*Above and right: Tony Blair and team review the coverage in
the last Sunday newspapers before polling day.*

Then he hit the road, either by bus, Jaguar or helicopter from Battersea heliport. Once, in the last week, he and Major almost ran into each other at Battersea as they both headed off to the marginal Tory seats that one man was defending from the other.

Blair - mostly through Campbell - was constantly in touch with Brown and Mandelson at Millbank. He himself spoke daily by phone to John Prescott, who topped 11,000 miles in what Labour claimed the longest campaign journey in the history of British politics. Robin Cook often spoke to Blair too, though not daily.

Though he stayed away overnight half a dozen times during his tour, Blair liked to get home. He rarely attended evening meetings at Millbank, though phone calls to Islington would continue till late. His staff say he has always been ruthless about getting home to see his family and has no patience with the culture of meet-ings-for-the-sake-of-meetings that some executives mistake for hard work.

He values his switch-off mechanism. One of the many pieces of advice he took from the Manchester United manager Alex Ferguson, a lifelong Labour man, was: "Don't make the mistake of thinking you have to work the whole time.

"Switch off. Take a break. Nip home to see the family. Get out of the bubble whenever you can."

Ferguson was a regular caller to Campbell's mobile, as Campbell revealed in a piece for the Mirror. Ferguson's experience as the manager of the club apparently coasting to the 1997 championship was appropriate for Blair. Ferguson told him he was 4-2 up with 20 minutes to go, the sort of position in which United would be getting players behind the ball and waiting for their opponents to make mistakes - "then we kill them". Although there are strains peculiar to being in front, it less tiring than trailing behind.

And there was another reason why Blair looked as though he was achieving the unlikely feat of enjoying the campaign. He had his wife with him. Couples as successful as the Blairs, working long hours in separate careers, do not see enough of each other. Now Tony and Cherie were often together all day - admittedly in a lot of company, but even in the unintimate melee of the campaign, the pleasure they got from each other was obvious to the most hardened cynic.

The main reason for Blair's stamina, though, had to be the adrenalin of approaching victory. All the way through, the moment might have come when it started to go wrong. But it hadn't happened - yet - and here he was, closing in on victory, still unthreatened by opponents or events. From mid-campaign - he was in Southampton on April 16 - he was sure he was going to win, despite his constant warnings against complacency, to himself as much as others. I nearly caught him out ten days before polling when he said: "I really think we're going to do this."

He quickly added: "I don't mean I think we are going to win, but that we should win this. If we don't, we don't."

This was a couple of hours before the ICM poll showed Labour's lead plummeting.

Had an anti-Labour trend set in at the stage, the Tories might still have won, as the Blair team acknowledged once it was all over. The Tories needed the poll lead on the final Sunday to be around ten per cent and then they might be

in with a chance. But the four polls published in the last Sunday papers of the Tory era showed Labour at between 47 and 53, the Tories between 29 and 32. This was the same range in which the two main contenders had remained throughout the campaign. The polls had not moved significantly, with the exception of a couple of rogues. The average Labour lead had drifted down from 22 points at the start of campaigning to 16 and was now going back up (the weighted average of the Sunday polls was 48.5 to 30, with the Liberal Democrats on 14.5 per cent.) Blair was ahead as Prime Minister, Labour was ahead on the economy - the two underlying indicators that had always been against Kinnock's Labour in 1992 and which the pollsters were now watching for signs of a dramatic shift. But there was no shift. These two indicators remained steady to the end.

No wonder the Tories were ceasing to pretend that they were still in the game. Stories were starting to appear about rifts and rows, the start of deliberately-placed stories that are the first signs of blame-shifting among the key players.

Major was said to be over-ruling Central Office on final-week strategy and Mawhinney was said to be falling out with Lord Saatchi, whose advertising flair had helped win four elections.

Worse, the contenders were getting restive as the first day of the rest of their careers approached. One was said to be looking up the cuttings on what Tony Blair had done five years ago, as a model of how a future leader should behave in defeat.

WE SWOOPED on middle England in a fleet of 11 helicopters, like something out of Apocalypse Now. It was Apocalypse Soon for the Tory Party and Tony Blair wanted to show he was stepping up the pace in search of every vote; hence the exciting, but slightly pointless, heli-ride to Derby for a hospital visit that could easily have been timed to suit the battlebus. Blair was greeted by a crowd waving purple flags and wearing purple hats. The buses, waiting on a football field, had been re-decorated purple. There was some debate about whether purple signified leadership, as for the Roman Emperors, or whether it was simply a favourite Blair colour from the days of purple loons when he sang with the Ugly Rumours at university. Perhaps Labour was simply going for the interior decorator vote.

The purple buses headed for Nottingham, for the latest Labour show. Tim Pigott-Smith, the actor who compered the evening, lived up to the high standard set by Patrick Stewart at the first of these events.

He quoted JK Galbraith, the American economist: "There are times in politics when you must be on the right side and lose."

"Well, we've done that," said Pigott-Smith. "Four times. This time, at last, I believe we are going to be on the right side and win."

It was rousing stuff and, when he introduced David Blunkett, the crowd roared its approval.

Blunkett told a story that put Blair's "education, education, education" theme into human form. It was about a boy from a poor home who left school at 16 without any qualifications , spent eight years at night school getting his O and A levels and , when he finally reached university, found the people there were no more intelligent than the people he grew up with. The boy was David Blunkett.

> "There are times in politics when you must be on the right side and lose. This time, at last, I believe we are going to be on the right side and win."

A Labour government had to conquer the low expectations in much of the education system, said Blunkett, and "if Tony gives me the job from this weekend, we will make a start".

He was followed by the Eastenders actor Ross Kemp, who was greeted by squeals of pleasure. By the time Kemp introduced Tony Blair, the audience was quite carried away. Blair was given a standing ovation before he spoke a word.

There is a fine line between enthusiasm and triumphalism. Blair was so anxious to avoid a repeat of the Sheffield rally, when triumphalism damaged Neil Kinnock, that "rally" was a banned word and these Labour shows were given uncomfortable titles like "an evening of entertainment and politics".

With the word "landslide" splashed across the front pages, Blair was determined not to look arrogant as the final week began.

He had intended to do another of his unscripted performances from the front of the stage. But, sensing the atmosphere, he stuck to the podium. It was a rare sight - a politician trying not to over-excite his audience.

"We approach these last few days with a sense of humility and a sense of responsibility, but a sense of excitement and hope, as well," said Blair.

How is a leader to conduct himself as he approaches near-certain victory? To be sure, triumphalism threatened to induce complacency among Labour supporters and nausea among the rest. But if the country was not going to get excitedly behind a vigorous young leader as he swept away an exhausted government, when would it?

Blair left the Royal Moat House Hotel, Nottingham, at 8am and went to the BBC for a Today programme interview with John Humphrys, whose irritatingly sterile questioning emphasised how little there was left to for anyone to say. Blair refused to be irritated, laughing at Humphrys' absurdly aggressive interruptions.

He caught up with his travelling media at Carlton TV's Nottingham studios, for a satellite link-up with Labour's daily press conference, chaired by Gordon Brown back at Millbank.

Blair was in playful mood, partly because of the slight weirdness of talking down the line to Labour's technicians, while his press pack wise-cracked in front of him.

"Am I looking into your camera, Simon?"

"Yes, you look wonderful."

"Simon, I like you too."

Gordon Brown's voice came down the line, opening the press conference, and then disappeared.

"I've lost it," Blair murmured.

Brown came back on line in time and, at his prompt, Blair launched into his theme for the day, the NHS.

"The NHS represents all the best of Labour and all the best of Britain. I fear for the future of the NHS if the Tories get back in".

He quoted that morning's Mirror, in which 59 eminent medical figures had called the Tories' internal market "a cancer eating away at the health service".

Blair and Brown took a mix of questions from the two audiences.

The first, from Michael Brunson of ITN, was another sign that there was nothing left to say to the nation. Don't you believe it's all over?

"This election is not over till it's over," said Blair. "I don't think this is a landslide country. As soon as you take the British people for granted, they quickly remind you who is boss."

He passed a question about the windfall tax to Brown. While the Shadow Chancellor was answering, disaster struck. The poster hanging behind Blair - "Vote, because Britain deserves better" - fell down. Blair turned and watched it settle on the studio floor. The laughter from Millbank could be heard down the line.

Blair grinned: "Thanks very much, guys."

When the press conference finished, he came down from the small stage and asked: "Can I say a word of thanks to whoever put the posters up? There's never one of these link-ups that goes without a mishap."

It was a good-natured complaint. He was in too good a mood to gripe. He would not have seen the funny side if the contest had been

tighter. The purple buses took Blair and camp followers to Loughborough and Leicester, where he gave the same message: "This is not a land-slide country. It isn't over till it's over. Come out and support us. Take nothing for granted."

While Blair pounded from marginal to marginal, John Major was flying to Northern Ireland, Wales and Scotland. His point was the defence of the United Kingdom, the theme he had always credited for turning the 1992 election. He did 1,000 miles in the day.

Those who travelled with the party leaders were often struck by the sheer pointlessness of the long journeys and short stops, by the poor ratio of miles covered to voters reached. On this epic trip, all Major managed in Wales was a 20-minute talk to activists in Anglesey while his travelling press sat in the bus at a layby waiting to go straight back to the airport.

Major finished his tour at Westminster. With Big Ben behind him, he spoke dramatically of the defence of the Union. The great clock just happened to be chiming six - news time. He said it was time to "draw a line in the sand" against those who would let our sovereignty go to Brussels and let Scottish independence break up the Union. The sand cliché was a reminder of happier times for Major, the Gulf War in his first months at Number Ten.

"So the message I would give to you and the British nation," he said to an audience of bravely cheering Central office staff, journalists who knew the game was up and tourists who had wandered into the odd world of British democracy, "the message is - you have 72 hours to save the Union, 72 hours in which to make sure that the system of government that has prevailed in this country for a very long time is protected and enshrined."

Senior Conservative sources had briefed a few hours before that their poll returns from the marginals were not as good as they had hoped at this stage.

For all his fighting talk, Major could not help a valedictory note creeping into his Big Ben speech (when a reporter had suggested a few days before that his campaign had a valedictory note, Major said: "Valedictory - that's a big word. I hope you can spell it."). The Prime Minister who had 72 hours to save his skin turned to his supporters and said: "I know how hard some of

*Cheers: Tony and Cherie Blair canvassing with
a cuppa.*

you have worked over the last few weeks. It's been a lot of fun.."

It was a paragraph that did not fit with the one before or the one after, as if by mistake he had allowed a draft of his election-night concession speech to slip out three days early.

ANYONE looking for that mythical country, Middle England, could do no better than head for the Gloucester Civil Service Club. Gloucester is the kind of place John Major must have been thinking of when he spoke of England as a country of "long shadows on county grounds, warm beer, invincible suburbs, dog lovers, old maids bicycling to Holy Communion through the morning mist."

It is one of the few memorable phrases Major put into the political language, even if he borrowed much of it from George Orwell. When he used the phrase, in 1993, Major's unspoken assumption was that the "invincible suburbs" would be forever Tory.

Now, on a sunny lunchtime in late April, the dog lovers and old maids of Middle England were gathered on the lawn of the Gloucester Civil Service Club for a barbecue, along with young mothers and pensioner couples. The guest of honour was the leader of the Labour Party.

It was an event soaked in symbolism. With the marquees and parasols and the jazz trio playing the sort of easy listening music you hear on Radio Two, it felt as though the Labour entourage had wandered by accident into a Tory garden party. In fact, it was a gathering of Tory supporters who had wandered into the Labour Party; and not by accident.

Here were the people - or, at least, a representative sample - whom Tony Blair had single-mindedly pursued ever since becoming party leader. It was as if, in election week, he had finally chased his quarry to this nice corner of England. It was the end of the hunt. The people of the invincible suburbs were ready to vote Labour.

Everyone at the Gloucester barbecue was an ex-Tory voter invited by the party canvassers who had tracked them physically while Blair

It was as if, in election week, he had finally chased his quarry to this nice corner of England. It was the end of the hunt. The people were ready to vote Labour.

was hunting them ideologically. Watching Blair speak to these people, there was a strong impression that he had always known this was where he was heading and precisely which route he would take. All the party reforms, the rhetorical revolution on the family, crime and tax, the ruthless elimination of the spending pledges that would frighten Middle England, the military organisation of the party machine, the careful selection of costed policies - all of it had fallen into place piece by piece so that Blair could stand on the terrace of Gloucester Civil Service Club and be among friends.

This was, of course, the seat which would give Labour a majority if it fell, which was why Blair had come back a second time. But there was more to his visit than that. These were Blair's people, the foundation stone of the New Labour coalition which he hoped would put him in power by the end of this gruelling week and maybe keep him there a long time if the Tories were foolish enough to let them go for good.

At the edge of the crowd politely seeking Blair's autograph, a teacher called Diana Jeynes explained why she was voting Labour: "I took early retirement, which was more or less enforced, when the school I was at had to cut its budget by £17,000. You don't do that by switching the lights off.

"I was devastated by what was going on in the education system, the lack of funding and the whole atmosphere - the government was undermining the teaching profession, making us feel like second class citizens.

"My number one reason for switching to Labour is the pledge on class sizes. I was teaching a reception class of 34 children.

"I have always voted Conservative until now, but I am totally disillusioned with them."

Those who looked down their noses at Blair's pledges under-estimated their power for

the disillusioned people of Middle England, who did not expect Utopia and would have quibbled at the price tag if Labour offered it. In Gloucestershire, 27 per cent of under-sevens are taught in classes of more than 30. That's a lot of teachers and parents who understand the power of the class-size pledge better than Blair's detractors.

From Gloucester, Blair was delayed on his way through Tory England by an IRA bomb threat that closed the M5. His next stop was Bristol. Again it was a second visit, but the local party was by now convinced it could take a big prize, William Waldegrave's Bristol West seat. This was not complacency, but a hard resolve to turn out every last voter and turn out every Tory possible. All across the country, 200 sitting MPs were going into their neighbouring marginals to lead the final push. Gordon Brown called it the most intensive piece of campaigning ever undertaken. Millbank Tower was virtually emptied of staff, who headed for the towns where doors needed knocking and lifts to polling booths organised.

In his speech at Bristol Council House, Blair promised a "radical government", while stressing that being radical did not mean turning the clock back. He accused Heseltine of arrogance for saying the country was "sleepwalking to disaster". The disaster would be a Tory fifth term and people had "woken up to it, " said Blair.

He spoke about "the great British dream", by which he meant that "each generation does better than the last". The difference between Labour and the Tories is that "we want it for all the people, not just a privileged few".

He concluded with a tribute to his predecessor. "John Smith said the night before he died: all we ask is the chance to serve".

Reassurance: Tony Blair needs to convince voters that there are no old fears with New Labour.

April 30
THE END OF
THE ROAD

TONY Blair was up early for the last day's campaigning. The red Jaguar picked him up at 6.30am. The first mile of the 639 he would travel that day was down to the Thames and across the river to GMTV. The second mile was back across and along the river to Millbank Tower for the final press conference, at 7.15am.

As well as the usual tea and coffee, there were bacon rolls and croissants for the hundreds of journalists. Getting up early added to the air of adventure. Whatever their politics, journalists love change because it is a better story and they were dying now to get on with the two great subplots of post-election politics, Labour in power and the Tories at war. Nobody was in any doubt about the result. In this atmosphere, the warrior against complacency faced a stiff test. He knew how hard any hint of smugness would be punished by the voters.

He made the mistake of cracking a joke in reply to one of the first questions. It was a harmless quip about his tie. Referring to a viewer who had criticised his blue tie on Election Call the day before, he said: "At least I'm wearing a red tie today."

In fact, it was more like the Mandelson purple of the stage backdrop and the press was taken by a fit of giggles. There was another when Elinor Goodman of Channel Four News made a slip of the tongue and asked about "the six months of this campaign".

When Blair was asked if he would feel a sense of anticipation as the polling booths closed, he could not resist a look of heavy irony, before saying: "It would be odd if there wasn't a mild sense of anticipation. I think that wouldn't be overdoing it."

Blair, who joined in the laughter, was worried that the whole jolly event might look too flip to TV viewers. He was having as much trouble as anyone fighting down the end-of-term feeling.

> I told him I had drawn
> 105, 115 and 129 in
> the battlebus sweep.
> "You've no chance
> with any of those," he
> said. He did not mean
> that they were too low.

He knew there was nothing more left to do now - too late to strike new themes or stake out new positions, too late to wrong-foot the Tories any more. He just had to be seen criss-crossing the country in search of every last vote, right to the end. And he had to avoid looking as if he was taking the voters for granted.

Released at last from the tyranny of tactical planning, he allowed himself the luxury of feeling demob happy as he headed out into the country one last time. When I interviewed him over breakfast on the plane from Stansted to Prestwick, he wanted only to chat and joke. He kept sending himself up whenever he caught himself saying the same things he had already said in more than 400 campaign interviews. For the candidate, the constant repetition of the key themes is a cruel and unusual punishment. Blair had heard and appreciated the joke among the travelling media, invented by Valentine Low of The Evening Standard: "Better criminals, Smaller hospitals, Shorter Jobs, Tough on pensioners..."

He got serious when I asked what had been his low point of the campaign. He said it was when the Tories dragged his children into the election, by making an issue of Euan's school, the Oratory. If the Conservatives could have seen his unforgiving look, they would have realised what a hard opponent they had taken on. This was something that many of them never did understand. They believed their own propaganda about him. Even now, on this final day, Major was trying to dismiss Blair as "well-packaged". The Conservatives never quite understood that, within the professional packaging, Tony Blair is a blade of cold steel. They still didn't realise it, even now that the blade was running them through.

He knew he'd won, though he refused to admit it for the record. But he didn't believe in a landslide. When I told him I'd drawn 105, 115 and 129 in the battlebus sweep on Labour's majority, he said: "You've no chance with any of those." He did

not mean they were too low. At Prestwick the Blairs, holding hands, transferred to a helicopter and flew to Dumfries, for a short speech in a sunny park. Then it was back in the helicopter for a stunning ride over Hadrian's Wall, to Darlington and a busride to Stockton, for the last of the town centre speeches, and on to the last school visit. Cherie joined the children singing Jerusalem.

Then it was on to Middlesborough, where Blair was greeted at a police station by the last celebrity of the campaign, Helen Mirren of Prime Suspect. The last car ride took him home to Trimdon.

On the press bus, we were given the final statistics for the tour - 9,168 miles, of which 1,633

were in the last five days. We had been to 60 constituencies, eaten 550 croissants and 1,800 bars of chocolate.

The buses pulled up at Trimdon Labour Club, the end of the road. John Burton was at the door to greet everyone like old friends. For the first time anyone could remember, the media were given a round of applause, by the Labour people packed in for the homecoming.

Tony Blair told them he couldn't have done anything without them and thanked them from the bottom of his heart. He went through, one last time, the speech he had given all over the country for 30 days and nights. He would never give this speech again. The next time he spoke in public, at

In their hands: Labour stressed its commitment to better schools.

his count, the nation's verdict would surely be clear and people would want to hear no more of Tory failure. All that would be over.

This was his last speech as leader of the Opposition, a job he had always wanted to escape as soon as possible because the only point of it was to move on. He was coming to the end of the last day on which he would ask himself what he would say rather than what he would do.

He was very close now to the power that had come to seem a Conservative monopoly. Just how close was underlined by some of the faces in the crowd, who were neither Trimdon people nor media. Tony Blair may be at home, but Special Branch had come indoors with the next Prime Minister. He would never again be without a security detail.

And at the back of the room stood Jonathan Powell, Blair's chief of staff. It was the first time Powell had been spotted on the tour. Throughout the campaign, he had been liaising with the head of the Civil Service, Sir Robin Butler, on the transition. Now Powell had come to brief his boss on the transfer of power, a ruthlessly instant process which Powell and Butler had choreographed in readiness for Friday lunchtime.

But first came the small matter of turning an opinion poll lead into votes.

"The very simple choice that people have got in this next 24 hours is this," said Tony Blair. This was his final soundbite for the last election bulletins.

"It is 24 hours to save our NHS, 24 hours to give our children the education they need, 24 hours to give hope to our young people, security to our elderly..."

When Blair and his team drove away from the Labour Club, with Jonathan Powell in the second car, the campaign was over and preparation for government had begun.

May 1
A NICE KIND
OF BASTARD

THE candidate woke on polling day with the rest of his life in the nation's hands. The final polls gave him a record election day lead, though Gallup showed signs of slippage, down by seven points to a mere 13. MORI was down by one to 20, Harris down one to 17 and ICM - a scary five a week ago - was back up to ten. Each was a landslide poll.

Euan, Nicky and Kathryn had come up to be with their father and mother. The first family, as they would now be perhaps until the children were all gone from home, walked across the fields to the polling booth.

Even now, with a few precious last hours off duty, Blair wore the white shirt of leadership. The supreme politician of his time, as his victory would make him, gave his children lessons in facing the right way for the cameras that they would have to get used to. Their lives would be public property from tomorrow. The Blairs went home still ordinary citizens, but only just.

In fact, Tony Blair was not off duty at all. Back home, he sat in the sunny garden with Jonathan Powell and Alastair Campbell, selecting Bills for the Labour government's first Queen's Speech and picking his Cabinet. The warrior against complacency had lost out to the incoming Prime Minister. The result had to be taken for granted if he wasn't to be overwhelmed when the decision-making started tomorrow afternoon.

Blair himself had well described the position he was now in, when talking to rugby-playing students at Loughborough on the campaign trail, about his memories of being a schoolboy fullback.

"The ball goes up in the air and , as you're waiting for it to come down, they're all piling in on you."

Now, as he waited for the ball to come down,

> People wanted to see him show he had passion and principles, so he was able to switch to his positive message earlier and with more conviction.

he insisted the prospect of being Prime Minister did not bring him out in a cold sweat - "I'm ready for it".

So he really was as confident as he looked? "No politician is as confident as he looks."

He still didn't believe there would be a landslide. He had told me his own eve-of-poll prediction was a majority of 30. The party's final private polling pointed to a majority of 41. Even a victory on the scale would have meant the biggest swing since the war. The evidence of the published opinion polls, all pointing to majorities of well over 100, went unheeded. It just couldn't happen.

Blair thought the Tories had got their campaign completely wrong. They had failed to see that if you are going to be negative you must also be credible. Their tax scares in 1992 had been credible. But by breaking their own tax promises they had ruined their credibility and the weapon had broken in their hand.

Major himself was to blame for this, no-one else. The problem was in his own psychology, as Blair saw it - Major had absolutely no faculty of self-criticism. He could not see the damage done by his tax betrayal because he was unable to be sufficiently honest with himself to accept that he had betrayed the voters. Without that self-criticism, Major could not grasp the problem he faced, never mind produce a remedy.

The thing that amazed Blair most about the Tory campaign was that it hadn't stuck to economic recovery. Britain may not be booming, but the economy was growing and that could have been exploited if the right language had been found. But the Conservative campaign kept wandering away from the economy. Blair thought this was because Ken Clarke - "the only one of them who has stood up for what he believes in" - was too marginalised by the Eurosceptics to play a full role. With a marginalised Chancellor, it is hard to make an issue of the economy. So

Europe had been decisive in that sense.

But also it had divided them. Tony Blair would always look back on the moment he heard about John Horam's revolt as the moment he knew he would be Prime Minister.

There was more to Labour's victory than Tory failure. Blair thought his own performance - too tense at first, he admitted - had picked up when he started talking more about what he believed in than about reassuring voters about what Labour no longer was.

Here too the Tories had helped him. By going for him as an empty candidate, they forced him to start being passionate about the changes he wanted to make to the country. It was all very well to say he should have done that from the start in any case. But he believed that if he had he done so, the uncommitted would have recoiled, concluding that Labour might still be too dangerous. He was convinced this fear still lurked beneath the surface. But the Tory attack made emptiness a greater peril for his campaign than dangerousness. People wanted to see him show he had passion and principles, so he was able to switch to his positive message earlier and with more conviction than otherwise.

Blair had been more alert to the risk of seeming to stand for nothing than his staff. While they thought the controversy over air traffic control was of little interest to the ordinary voter, Blair thought it was damaging . The staff were right to the extent that it did not move the polls. But Blair sensed a wider problem than the technicalities of selling traffic control - the U-turn charge was undercutting his appeal for trust. He realised had to show what he stood for if he was to ask for trust. Going positive - as Campbell had said he would, in his Milton Keynes briefing - was Blair's personal decision. He felt relaxed with himself from then on.

He thought his unscripted speeches had brought his campaign to life. Although Edinburgh had been the first time the media noticed the change in him, he traced it back a week earlier to Plymouth, when he went off script for an extended peroration. There, he found the tone and style he needed. The Edinburgh speech was the one where he got it just right and from then on he decided to keep making more or less the same speech. He was pleased that his travelling media could recite the main passages, because that suggested the message was getting through. His own gathering momentum after Edinburgh coincided with the Tory Party's nervous breakdown over Europe.

He and his Millbank team waited and waited for the Tories to launch the counter-attack. They had expected the Tories to try to "separate the head from the body" - that is, portray Blair as totally different from his party. Preparations were made for the trouble that would follow if the Tories succeeded in niggling John Prescott, Clare Short or Robin Cook into saying something that "separated the head from the body".

The Tories never made a serious try at it. Besides, everyone was too self-disciplined, so that the Conservatives were reduced to complaining that Blair had gagged his party. Here again the Conservatives under-estimated their opponents. Blair was not the only one who had learned lessons from successive defeats. Prescott, incidentally, had a Tory gaffe-watch team devoted entirely to his campaign. It was pulled off after three weeks because it was a waste of time.

The Labour high command was forced to conclude that the Tories were not as clever as they believed themselves to be. They had spent years depriving themselves of their most reliable weapons and found no new ones. The recession deprived them of competence. Broken promises deprived them of trust. The Lamont-Clarke budgets deprived them of tax. They came up with nothing new and failed to exploit the one thing going for them, economic growth.

Their "Britain is Booming" ads were a disaster. Labour's private polling showed this so clearly and promptly that Blair's team were left wondering why the Tories had not themselves gone to the trouble of asking their pollsters to market test the slogan.

When Labour's pollsters asked people to judge between "Britain is Booming" and "Britain deserves better", Labour's slogan won by 84 points to seven. The Tories made the mistake of so overstating their case that they made it unbelievable.

Labour's market research also showed, at the height of the Tory Euro-crisis, that weak leadership was making more impact than Euroscepticism.

Labour's devotion to market research -

Tony Blair and John Prescott meet the crowds in Stockton-on-Tees.

polling, focus groups and so forth - was often scorned. But politics is not a game of blind man's buff. Tony Blair always tested his instincts against measurable evidence.

Maybe his instincts were better than Major's anyway, but the Labour leader's painstaking methods proved more successful than Major's insistence on running his campaign by gut feeling.

The Conservatives and their leader made mistake after mistake. Did they matter, or are elections won and lost over the years in power rather than the weeks on the road?

Tony Blair's view was that, whatever difference Labour's campaign successes did or didn't make, a botched Labour campaign might have let the Tories back in.

In the end, Labour's secret weapon was their most visible one - Blair himself. Labour could not have won had it not at last been led by a potential Prime Minister, rather than a first-class Opposition leader, which Neil Kinnock had been.

John Smith had been a potential Prime Minister and one of the saddest things about the campaign was that his name was so little heard. Tony Blair had campaigned on trust; it was John Smith who had first sown a sense of trust in Labour, which Tony Blair was now reaping, brilliantly.

There is no point in debating whether John Smith would have won. Tony Blair had always known that he would need to do it a different way. Where John Smith could be solid, Blair had to be daring, ruthless, constantly in action. It

*On our way:
Victory is in
the air.*

*All together now: the Blair family
goes to the polls.*

was a very long time since anyone had called him Bambi. Alastair Campbell had a better description, from an Australian magazine that understood Blair better than the Tories: "A nice kind of bastard".

ELECTION night was like a dream through which Tony Blair, his family, friends and team went in fear of waking to find it wasn't true.

The candidate waited at home in Trimdon for the polls to close on his victory. He wore jeans, slippers, a blue and green rugby shirt. The curtains were drawn against the cameramen and wellwishers. At 10pm the phone rang. Blair himself took the call, so he missed the moment when the BBC announced its dreamlike exit poll, showing Labour leading the Conservatives by 47 points to 29, a swing of 12 per cent. Labour needed a swing of fractionally more than four. Whatever the margin of error, the exit poll must mean a comfortable victory.

The poll was, in fact, no surprise, because Campbell had learned during the afternoon that it was showing Labour's percentage lead running in double figures. Back at Millbank, party pollster Philip Gould had revised his estimate of Labour's majority dramatically upwards during the day. His final prediction was a majority of at least 100, but he was greeted with disbelief. Blair himself wanted some real facts from real counts.

The first result came from a safe Labour seat, Sunderland South. Chris Mullin had held it with a swing from the Tories of 10.5 per cent.

It was at this point that Blair's team of warriors against complacency, even the veterans who had never got over the dashed hopes of 1992, knew they were safe to savour the moment. It was going to happen - unless it was all a dream.

Blair was the quietest person among the family crowded into the house, all of them bubbling and cheering , except the candidate. He was preparing what he would say in the speech-

The warrior against complacency could lay down his disbelief and abandon himself to the thrill of victory. The country had given him one of the greatest triumphs in political history.

es that lay ahead on the night of victory - at his count, at Trimdon Labour Club, at the Labour celebrations at the Royal Festival Hall.

He changed into the uniform of leadership and left for the count, even at this stage keeping up a non-complacent front for the TV cameras: "Let's wait and see," he said.

At Newton Aycliffe leisure centre, he went to a backroom with Cherie, the children, Tony's father and both Cherie's parents. By the time the Sedgefield result was ready, Labour had scored stunning victories in Birmingham Edgbaston, Portsmouth North and the capital of Thatcher's Britain, Basildon. Euan was following closely, asking what the Edgbaston swing had been. Blair himself kept muttering terms of disbelief: "It's not real...this can't be happening."

The family came out on to the floor of the count and stood waiting for Tony to go up on stage with Cherie and his agent, John Burton. Cherie kissed Tony's father, Leo. Her father, Tony Booth, chattered excitedly.

The magnitude of Labour's victory was clear now. Maybe that explained the subdued tone of Blair's short speech after his own result was declared. He seemed awed by the scale of events.

He thanked Cherie, as "a wonderful source of support"; his father, for being "magnificent to me all through my life"; and said "all that could make this complete was that my mother was here still".

The police, whom he thanked for their work in "these slightly unusual circumstances", escorted him across the constituency to Trimdon, where John Major rang to say he would shortly be making a statement conceding defeat.

The incoming Prime Minister was now behind schedule. Trimdon Labour Club could hardly wait for its big moment, knowing from the giant screen on stage that its man had long left Newton Aycliffe. The place was packed, the atmosphere a cross between a sauna and a soccer match. Every Labour gain was cheered like a goal. The biggest greeted the prediction by Lance Price of the BBC that Michael Portillo was about to go down at Enfield Southgate.

An even bigger cheer greeted Tony and Cherie when at last they were escorted into the crowd by John Burton. Tony Blair had to wait some time for a hearing.

"You know me, I am never complacent, but it's looking very good," he said.

He looked glazed - tired now, stunned by the enormity of his achievement, quiet at the centre of the whirlwind he had unleashed. Dignity must be hard work when your instincts are to punch the air in glee. But down among the crowd, as he battled his way out to head for London, he let his boyish delight show as he grinned with unrestrained excitement and shook old friends by the hand. Cherie followed him out, hugging and kissing.

They were driven through the dark to Teesside airport, following the results on the car radio. Neil Hamilton was beaten, the Tories wiped out in Scotland and Wales. As the Blairs neared the airport, so Labour neared its majority. Already, 300 seats had been won and the Tories were barely into double figures.

On the plane to London, they were kept in touch with results by party HQ, paging Alastair Campbell. When confirmation of Portillo's defeat came up on the pager just after 3am, they thought it might be someone's idea of a joke. When they accepted it was true, they knew they had a result for which "landslide" was an understatement. The warrior against complacency could at last lay down his disbelief and abandon himself to the thrill of victory. He was flying high over a country that had given him one of the greatest triumphs in political history. By the time his plane landed, Labour had won the 330 seats needed to form a government. It had happened. They were not dreaming.

At Stansted, Tony Blair paused in his victory dash to London. He was heading for Labour's celebration party at the Royal Festival Hall with two small planeloads of family, Trimdon friends and staff. He waited for the second plane to land

because he wanted them all there for his victory speech and knew how much it meant to them that they should be.

Finally, Blair's entourage headed into London in two buses and a fleet of cars, under a sliver of moon. When they stopped at a traffic light, Blair waved from his Daimler at his staff. They crowded at the window of their bus, taking pictures of the man who would never be so close to them again, once the machinery of power took him over. Some of them had worked for Neil Kinnock, who had never managed to escape from the intimacy of campaigning to the distance of power. At that moment, by the traffic lights, Kinnock was on the radio, choking with emotion at his pleasure in this young protégé's dreamlike success. Together, Kinnock's emotion and Blair's victory wave made for a moment of intense poignancy, before the lights turned green and the conqueror sped on into his capital.

The winner took a congratulatory call from President Clinton. In these hours, Tony Blair was in a no-man's land between candidate and statesman.

He came into London with the sun coming up. At 5.12am, his convoy crossed the river with St. Paul's glowing pink in the dawn. The lighted front of the Festival Hall was draped in red banners, a revolutionary piece of symbolism that Labour could dare to indulge in, now that victory was accomplished.

As the buses and cars pulled up, the dawn was full of music: "Things Can Only Get Better".

The screen on the stage that awaited the leader flashed up the message: "New Labour, New Government." Shadow Ministers, who would soon be emerging from the shadows into government, allowed themselves the luxury of laughing at the unimaginable scale of Labour's win. They were intoxicated by the unthinkable majorities at their own counts.

Robin Cook, deadpan as usual, noted with quiet pleasure that his controversial prediction of a landslide had been something of an understatement.

Tony Blair had trouble making his victory speech heard amid the din of relief, as much as triumphalism, that greeted the man who had at last delivered Labour from the long night of Opposition.

"A new dawn has broken," he said. "Isn't it wonderful? We always said that if we had the courage to change we could do it and we did it.

"The British people have put their trust in us. It is a moving and humbling experience. The size of our likely majority now imposes a special responsibility on us. We have been elected as New Labour and we will govern as New Labour.

"We were elected because as a party today we represent the whole of this nation and we will govern for the whole of this nation, every single day. We will speak up for that decent , hardworking majority of the British people whose voices have been silent for too long and we will set about doing the good, practical things that need to be done - extending educational opportunity, not to an elite, but to all our children, modernising our welfare state, re-building our National Health Service as a proper national health service.

"We will work with business to create the dynamic and enterprising economy we will need. We will work for all our people to create that just and decent society the British people have wanted for so long.

"This vote tonight has been a vote for the future, for a new era of politics in Britain. So let us put behind us the battles of this last century and address the new challenge of this new century, when we build a nation united, with no-one shut out, no-one excluded.

"That is the country we have wanted for so long, a country whose politics live up to the finest ideals of public service and a Britain that stands tall in the world, whose sense of its

You've done it: Leo Blair congratulates his son and daughter-in-law.

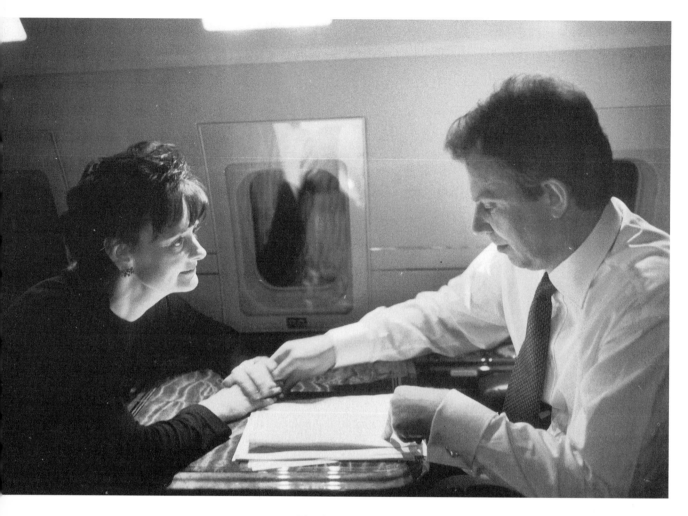

*The Blairs on their flight to victory. Beneath
them the country was experiencing
a landslide.*

future is as certain and confident as its sense of its own history.

"We have won support in this election from all walks of life, all classes of people, every corner of our country. We are now today the people's party, the party of all the people, the many not the few, the party that belongs to every part of Britain.

"I want everyone to feel proud of their country tonight because everyone has a stake in its success. Tonight the people of Britain are uniting behind new Labour, they are uniting around decent British values, uniting to face the challenge of the future, uniting at long last as one nation.

"Three days ago I quoted John Smith. He said - all we ask is the chance to serve. Tonight the British people have given us the chance to serve and serve we will with all our heart.

"We say tonight - you the British people

Awesome: the scale of the victory starts to
sink in for Tony Blair on the plane.
Following pages: Scenes of jubilation at the
Royal Festival Hall as a new era dawns for
Britain.

have given us the chance to serve, you have put your trust in us. We say to you - we shall repay that trust.

"We have been people saying, but never given the chance to do and yet the only purpose of being in politics is to make things happen. Now we have the chance to make things happen,

"We take that responsibility upon us. We will discharge it and we shall make this country as proud of us as tonight we are proud of them."

Beyond the security barriers that enclosed the hundreds of guests, every walkway, staircase and balcony of the South Bank complex was lined with revellers cheering and chanting. As the victors left they were greeted at the door by a roaring crowd that made it feel as though the revolution had come, which it had. By now, 6am, the longest period of one-party rule since universal suffrage was over and the party of power laid waste.

THE Tory years ended on Day 6,573 at 11.25am, when John Major came out of Number Ten, looked round to make sure Norma was with him, and went to the microphone.

"It has been an immense privilege to serve as Prime Minister of the United Kingdom," he said. He had delivered "benevolent improvements in the interests of all the people of this country". The incoming government, which he congratulated, would inherit "the most benevolent set of economic statistics of any incoming government since the First World War". He very much hoped the new government would be "successful in retaining this economy".

There was one thing he wanted to clear up. "When the curtain falls it is time to get off the stage and that is what I propose to do". He would advise his parliamentary colleagues to select a new leader. Now he was off to the Palace and then to the Oval to watch some cricket.

The Prime Minister's driver switched on the Daimler's engine. John Major waved to the staff at the windows - no longer his staff. He clasped Brian Mawhinney's hand and for a moment it looked as though Mawhinney might cry.

The Majors got in the official car for the last time and were driven away. Their children, James and Elizabeth, walked off towards Whitehall with their partners.

An era ended as Mawhinney, the party chairman, and Howell James, Major's political advisor, trudged the length of Downing Street and went out through the gates, the last Tories to leave the seat of power.

For a couple of hours, Number Ten was untenanted. The upstairs windows were wide open, as if to let in fresh air. Gradually the street began to fill with Labour staff, given time off to

The Majors got in the official car for the last time and were driven away. Number Ten was untenanted. The upstairs windows were open, as if to let in fresh air.

come and savour the moment they had worked for. They brought Union Jacks - New Labour's detailed attention to imagery had not deserted it now the victory was won.

Some of the older hands confessed they had never been in Downing Street before, so long had Labour been out of office. The younger Blairites made their way confidently to the citadel. The first to cross the threshold was Tim Allan, the very model of fresh-faced Blairism, followed by Hilary Coffman, who had worked for John Smith, Neil Kinnock and Michael Foot. They were Alastair Campbell's advance guard, press officers come to liase with Jonathan Haslam, the civil servant who had served as Major's press secretary.

At 1.03 the cheering and flagwaving began as the Prime Minister's Daimler returned from the Palace and out stepped Tony Blair. As he and Cherie made their slow, handshaking way up the street of power, two men hurried ahead. Alex Allan, the Prime Minister's principal private secretary, had gone to the Palace as a civil servant working for John Major and was now back with the Blair entourage, headed by Jonathan Powell. Allan and Powell went in together with the air of men with work to do when their chief had done with the crowds.

Tony Blair worked his way up the street more quickly than Cherie, as if he wanted to get on with government.

First he had one last speech to make, right at the end of the long road to Number Ten.

He stepped up to the podium left behind by John Major, to whom he paid tribute for the manner of his leaving. There was no other reference to the Tories. They were history and now Tony Blair was leader of the whole country first, of his party second.

His victory, he said, was "not a mandate for

*Above: Tony Blair's progress through the ecstatic
crowds in Downing Street. Below: The family
gather on the steps of Number Ten*

dogma or doctrine", but to do the things that
"desperately need doing". He would govern in
the interests of all the people. He would set his
government the objective of creating a world
class education system, of modernising the welfare state and the National Health Service, of
working in partnership with business to create a
competitive economy. "It will be a government
that seeks to restore trust in politics," he said.

It would "give this country strength and confidence in leadership both at home and abroad,
particularly in respect of Europe".

It would be "a government of practical measures in pursuit of noble causes."

Above all, he said, "we have secured a mandate to bring this nation together, to unite us -
one Britain, one nation in which our ambition
for ourselves is matched by our sense of compassion and decency and duty towards other
people. Simple values, but the right ones. For 18

Hall of fame: Tony and Cherie Blair join premiers of
the past on the staircase at 10 Downing Street

years - 18 long years - my party has been in Opposition. It could only say, it could not do. Today we are charged with the deep responsibility of government. Today, enough of talking - it is time now to do."

But , before he could do, there were pictures to be taken, the pictures that many in his party had despaired of ever seeing - a Labour Prime Minister on the doorstep of Number Ten. The first family posed and posed again, seeming happy to linger in the light of the flashguns, savouring this moment.

Finally, at 1.18pm on Day One of the new Labour government, Euan Blair stepped inside Number Ten, followed by Nicky, Kathryn, Cherie and, at last, Prime Minister Tony Blair.